NATO and the Middle East

NATO and the Middle East

The Making of a Partnership

ALESSANDRO MINUTO-RIZZO

NEW ACADEMIA
PUBLISHING

VELLUM

Washington DC

Library of Congress Control Number: 2017962355
ISBN 978-0-9995572-3-5 paperback (alk. paper)

VELLUM An imprint of New Academia Publishing

NAP
NEW ACADEMIA
PUBLISHING
New Academia Publishing, 4401-A Connecticut Ave. NW, #236,
Washington, DC 20008
info@newacademia.com - www.newacademia.com

For Gabriele, my cherished grandson, with love

Contents

Foreword

"NATO - out of area or out of business" said some of the cynics after the collapse of Communism, as if the absence of the previous enemy proved that the Alliance had fulfilled its collective defence task and was looking for a new role. In fact, the job of NATO was far from over with the end of the USSR and the Warsaw Pact.

Given that the primary purpose of the Atlantic Alliance was to protect the safety and security of its member states, a disorganized post-Soviet space would have been a real threat to the West's neighbourhood and indeed to the wider world. That is why wise and enlightened Western leaders saw a new role for the Alliance in helping the ordered transition of the Communist states to democracy, mixed economies, and civilian control of the military.

Then when the flames of the Balkan wars started in the eighties and peaceful mediation proved inadequate, it was the old Cold War Alliance which fired its first ever shots in anger to save Moslems from brutal ethnic cleansing. "Out of area" indeed, but in action to protect the NATO membership from the spill-over effects of the killing in Bosnia. It was the same four years later in Kosovo, as Milosevic outraged human decency and endangered regional stability with the killing and expelling of Kosovo's Albanian (Moslem) population.

Over the years since the old enemy of the Soviet Union disappeared, NATO has seen, on behalf of its expanding membership, the safety and security of its members threatened from much further away than just their physical borders. Terrorism organized in Afghanistan hit New York and piracy in the Indian Ocean attacked European shipping; NATO addressed both.

The story in this book chronicles another attempt by the Alliance to protect its members from instability, this time in the Arab world, by spreading the lessons of NATO's contribution to a stable and prosperous Trans-Atlantic space.

Deputy NATO Secretary General Minuto-Rizzo was given the mission to explore how NATO and the countries of the Middle East and North Africa (MENA as they are collectively known) could cooperate against modern threats which affect all countries. It was a tough task, but one for which his life as an Italian diplomat easily suited him. When I chose Alessandro as my Deputy I felt I had with me a distinguished and experienced diplomat of character and ability. I was not wrong, as this little memoir amply proves. He was also a good friend and a genuinely fine colleague.

The countries of MENA are, in truth, even more fractious and capricious than the countries of NATO - and that is some test. Getting consensus in NATO at 19 – as I had to do — and at 28, as Jens Stoltenberg has to do, is a monumental task. Getting the MENA countries round a table, and recognizing they had a common set of problems was close to impossible. But it had to be attempted. The stability of the MENA region is too important to all of us to ignore.

Here, in this book is a candid and colourful account of Alessandro's travels and encounters. Nobody reading it can fault the efforts he made and few can quibble at the level of success he had in forging a new NATO relationship to accompany the ones it has with Partner nations and Russia and Ukraine. It was a formidable achievement and it has well outlived his own tenure at NATO Headquarters.

The region, as I know travelling there myself these days, is going through an era of dramatic change. The Alliance can, and will help shape the outcome of that change. And that will be in the interests of those who live there as well as those who, at distance, are affected by it.

Rt Hon Lord Robertson of Port Ellen KT GCMG HonFRSE PC
Secretary General of NATO, 1999-2004

Acknowledgements

After beginning this volume, I realized it was a much more complicated story than I originally had believed. It was not intended to be merely a personal account, but neither was it to be a political analysis, which might be considered too scholarly and only for specialists. Furthermore, the Arab Spring had caught me in mid-stream and it was impossible to ignore.

I had in mind to write a factual description of why and how NATO took an interest in the southern shores of the Mediterranean, the Levant, and the Gulf. At the same time, my firm intention was not to bore the reader, and to bring as much life as possible to those events and to the many different people with whom I met. As a matter of fact, they are the real actors in this book that grew around them.

I therefore asked for the help of several friends, to whom I am sincerely grateful. Being a good journalist, Aldo Bagnalasta was patient enough to read successive versions and provide me with friendly and astute advice, including grammatical changes. Paolo Bacchielli helped me prioritize, and his experience as a European official was most useful in providing an overview.

I am very grateful to my nephew Giuliano De Giorgio for his valuable opinions and for having encouraged me to examine the subject of multilateralism in greater depth. He is on his second diplomatic assignment, and I wish him much luck and success!

I would also like to thank Mauro Battocchi and Carlo Jean for their friendship and for their support. Likewise, Alessandro Politi and Mario Arpino. A special note of gratitude goes to Luigi Cucca and Linda Lucinio who have given me constant and sensitive support at Enel during the editorial stages. To both my very best wishes.

This book would not have been possible if the Secretary General of the Atlantic Alliance had not placed complete trust in me, virtually giving me carte blanche. After Lord Robertson, a natural leader and a man of principle with special human qualities, who selected me as Deputy Secretary General, I must thank his successor, the Netherlands' Jaap de Hoop Scheffer, a true believer in Europe and in the transatlantic bond, as well as a leader and gentleman, without whose strong support things would have been very different. I am proud of their friendship.

The same goes for the members of the North Atlantic Council (NAC), NATO's highest decision-making body, during my years of service to the Alliance. They were the most remarkable group of ambassadors one could ever hope to meet, projecting both great authority and the highest mutual respect. I have to thank everyone for the flexible operational mandates and constant support I received.

In the Gulf region my first point of contact was the very able Sheikh Thamer Al-Sabah in Kuwait, a remarkable personality. Minister Mohammed Al-Rumaihi was of enormous help in Doha. In Morocco Youssef Amrani was the best friend I could count on. In Egypt Ahmed Aboul Gheit , Minister of Foreign Affairs and now Secretari General of the Arab League.

I also must mention and thank the then Crown Prince of Qatar (currently the Emir) and the Crown Prince of Bahrain for their kindness and the consideration shown to me at the end of my mandate.

My primary contacts were above all the Arab and Israeli ambassadors in Brussels.

It is difficult to name them all, but I especially would like to thank: Egypt's very able Mahmoud Karem; Ahmad Masa'adeh, the dynamic Jordanian representative; Israel's Oded Eran, who did his best to explain Jerusalem to me; the young Meshal Al-Thani from Qatar; Halim Benatallah from Algeria, with whom I was able to dribble many political problems; Nabeela Al-Mulla, a lady full of energy and a friend, ambassador of Kuwait. I remain in touch with most of them.

For my frequent trips, I especially relied on the Private Office of the Secretary General of NATO, as well as the International Staff's

Public Diplomacy and Political Affairs offices. My particular thanks go to: Nicola De Santis, an indispensable driving force of great professional ability; Thomas Wagner, whose political sensitivity was of great help; Alberto Bin, who provided an important point of continuity. Recognition is also due to Dominique Vanmarsnille, my most valuable assistant, as well as to my drivers Marc Van Hassel and André Bastin. We spent many hours together, becoming friends. The International Staff has many diverse individuals, and I was pleased to be counted as one of them. A wide world always has added value.

My gratitude is due also to Burcu San, Carmen Romero, Michel Soula, Ernst Reichl, and Hans-Christian von Reibniz, for their assistance in Brussels and abroad. The "close protection team," my companions on these unprecedented missions, also deserve my thanks, which I extend to Simon Philippe on behalf of them all.

The burgeoning activities with Middle Eastern partners of the NATO Defense College Foundation, which I help found and over which I have the pleasure to preside, have encouraged me to prepare this new substantially expanded, English-language edition of the book.

The American edition proves that sometimes luck may be on our side. I could not have found better editors than Deborah Park and Eric Terzuolo. Deborah has improved the text in a substantial way. Without her help, many words could have been misunderstood in a difficult political context. Eric has added a diplomatic and intellectual touch of high quality. In the end, I consider him to be more a partner than an editor.

I also owe special thanks to Anna Lawton, a very capable and fair publisher, for her generosity and for the methodology practiced by New Academia.

Finally, my family has been of invaluable support and encouragement. Gabriella for her great patience over time in seeing me work in unlikely situations, while on holiday, during the weekends, and on different continents, and who provided me with wise editorial advice. All my thanks go to Andrea and Alberto for their much-appreciated active and continuous support . Their affection has been of great encouragement to me, and they have always been in my heart during long hours of work.

Overview

History shows that we lived for millennia in isolated communities, having very little contact with one another. Although the passing of time saw the gradual formation of political entities, they initially had very little knowledge of each other and of the world in general. Today the situation is completely the reverse. Indeed, we have reached the point where, unless we jointly address the great challenges now facing us, our very survival is in jeopardy. The search for a wider base of consensus among the different regions of the world is the main theme and underlying reason for this book. It is an important subject for our times.

We are now living in a tightly knit interactive global society, in which it has become imperative to provide co-operative responses, and for which political stability is a decisive prerequisite. However, the world is far from enjoying a state of natural equilibrium, and is continually assailed not only by conflicting emotions and perceptions, but also by divergent interests. The awakening of peoples who were taken for granted until only very recently adds to the complexity. Moreover, we are aware that rational behavior by human beings, and also by governments, is not the rule.

Our starting point is that great area experts sometimes call the "arc of crisis," which extends from the Atlantic coast of North Africa to Central Asia and Pakistan, crossing Egypt, the Arabian Peninsula, and the Caucasus. This is the most difficult area in the world; its potential for destabilization far exceeds that found in any other part of the globe. However, any similarity ends there, because each country has its own characteristics, from Morocco to Egypt, to the Arabian Peninsula and the mountains of Yemen, the mythical kingdom of the Queen of Sheba.

It is a highly dangerous cocktail to handle and seems perpetually likely to explode. What is needed, and still lacking, is an international community able to manage the situation, with common objectives not motivated by seeking and concluding good business deals, securing oil, or containing the power of the Iranian ayatollahs. Many things come to mind, including perhaps a nostalgia that should not be confessed for the Cold War, which basically maintained a balance in world affairs and could easily be explained to everyone.

At the time this story begins, it was difficult to speak of any genuine cooperation that was beneficial for all parties concerned. These were times that saw car bombs continually exploding in the markets of Iraq, not to mention the war in Lebanon, Hamas, the Intifada, Gaza, and so on.

The natural conclusion is that, like the Balkans, this region has produced far more history than it has been able to consume. The Israeli-Palestinian crisis, for example, was an unavoidable theme in conversations held in any Arab capital, an irresolvable conflict that absorbed everyone's emotions, creating a sense of impotence and frustration, the cost of which was impossible to calculate.

As I experienced frequently in the period described here, from Morocco to Oman it was difficult to promote political projects on security issues and have them accepted. Opening doors and windows that have been closed for so long is a complex business. Yet we must move forward with the tools available, not those we dream of having if the world were different.

Here I may add, however, that as a result of my travelling along many roads from the Maghreb to Israel, and as far as the countries of the Gulf, I realized there also were facts pointing to a new arc of opportunities. Before our very eyes we could see an arduous search for reconciliation between tradition and modernity, via a process of change that, until the Arab Spring, admittedly was far too slow, and then suddenly took us by surprise. At the end of 2010, the Arab world appeared to have awakened and to be surging forward. Some years later, however, the hopes raised by what the ubiquitous Al Jazeera news service actually termed the "Arab Revolt" have been to a significant degree disappointed. Events seem to have moved far faster than our ability to chronicle them in books.

It is no accident that I mention Al Jazeera. It is the means by which we have seen the crowds marching in the streets of the Yemen, Tahrir Square at the height of tension, the population of Benghazi in jubilation for the choices they had made, and the bloody repression in Syrian cities and towns. I hesitate in fact to refer to these events as a "spring," suggesting an impersonal changing of the seasons, when in most cases we witnessed power systems being challenged by their own people.

Comparisons have been made to the fall of communism and of the Soviet Union, but here we are talking about situations for which no clear parallel to those events can be made. What instantly come to my mind are the protests that swept over Europe in 1848. These were popular movements calling for constitutions and the end of the absolute power of monarchies.

Whatever the precise definition, though, we know that some things have changed profoundly. Even in the field of global strategy, important things have taken place, although with less fanfare than one might have expected, given the convergence of many disparate events. In Libya in 2011, for example, the Atlantic Alliance was given the task of implementing a UN Security Council resolution: the very first NATO operation to be carried out on Arab soil. Another great novelty was that this took place with the express approval of the Arab League and the Gulf Cooperation Council. Qatar, the United Arab Emirates, Jordan, and Morocco actively took part, the first two using Italian military bases. The North Atlantic Council, the Alliance's highest decision-making body, was enlarged on this occasion to include these four countries, an unprecedented step.

But perhaps, for some perspective, we should take a step back and describe the international scene before September 2001. At that time, the Alliance was at the apex of its prestige, having won the Cold War, a clash of civilizations, in which the Warsaw Pact collapsed like a house of sand in March 1991. Then NATO successfully dealt with three serious crises in the Balkans — Bosnia, Kosovo, and Macedonia — where the United Nations and a united Europe had visibly failed. Indeed, while this was going on, the European Union's institutions were almost invisible. As a result, however, of the 1999 Kosovo campaign, which exposed their technological weakness, there was an attempt on the part of the EU leadership to put together some form of common defense policy. Another view was expressed by some well-known writers, such as Francis Fukuyama, according to whom History with a capital "H" was over and done with, and we were entering an indefinite period of peace.

These writers were abruptly silenced when, on live television, millions of people witnessed planes head towards the two most beautiful skyscrapers in New York and raze them to the ground. There was even greater surprise when it became known that the entire mission had been planned from distant highlands in south-central Asia, areas that were still unfamiliar in most Western capitals. This brought about a kind of death of geography: we no longer felt protected, as we had in the past, by distance, seas, and mountains. Consequently, 9/11 marked a historic watershed.

The US responded forcefully with every means it had. Considered a "war on terror," so began the hunt for Osama bin Laden that was to end ten years later. At the same time, misunderstandings and stereotypes started to appear, including that of all too often equating Islam with terrorism. The Afghan crisis continues to this day, and prospects for a peaceful conclusion appear dim. It seems like a sort of bad dream, but it is all too real. It is also an example of problems that can afflict other weak, failing, or failed states, and how daunting the challenges of creating security in such places can be.

This sets the stage for our story of NATO's response to the drama of September 2001, which included establishing a partnership between the Euro-Atlantic community and the countries of the Southern Mediterranean and the Persian Gulf. This was intended to extend collective security to these areas of the world. But why these countries in particular? Basically, because it was believed that only by engaging core Islamic countries could international security be guaranteed. The Atlantic Alliance, therefore, set out along the path of cooperative security. In other words, creating links among diverse and distant players, facing shared threats and with common interests. With what concrete objective? To put it simply, to bring these countries on board in an attempt to design a more equally shared world architecture. Obviously, this was not an easy goal, success was by no means assured, and even the final objectives were not fully defined.

Therefore, this is a story that has the Middle East, with its intermittent crises, as its stage, seen through the optic of NATO, the quintessentially Western institution, Euro-American at its core, that specializes in foreign and defense policy, which by their very nature are difficult as well as controversial. What makes this story interesting also is the novelty of the approach, and the effort made in those years to find, not without difficulty, a way to square the circle. This was an experiment I considered an important cause to which to dedicate myself.

However, this is the way of the future for managing global stability. The world is becoming increasingly complex, and there is no longer a dominant power. Productive dialogue among different peoples and cultures is essential, especially because never before in human history has interaction been as great as it is today. This change was inevitable, given that today's world is larger, colonialism is a thing of the past, pure power politics no longer pay off, and so-called coalitions of the willing are short-lived.

This book is based on the perspective of an organization that acts through consensus; in other words, it only takes decisions if the governments that comprise it are in agreement. This is why it is a political story, written in the modest hope of better explaining the complex nature of international action in our times.

Why write in the first person? As Deputy Secretary General of the Atlantic Alliance, for several years I was charged with initiating and promoting dialogue with the Arab countries of the Mediterranean and the Gulf, plus Israel. I could not have had a better assignment. It gave me great personal and professional satisfaction, enabling me to broaden my knowledge, not only of issues, but also of people, through experiences that otherwise would have been impossible. The events that have taken place since a young Tunisian fruit vendor, Mohammed Bouazizi, set himself on fire in December 2010 have reminded us of how enhanced dialogue and mutual understanding are extremely important for today, and given us a sense of the complexity of the issues, while raising many questions about the past and the future.

I recognize that it is impossible to recount THE history of something! In politics, as in personal life, there is never just one version. All depends on one's point of view, and the way you personally experience the situation. It is an undefined sum of factors that everyone views in a different light.

It is thus not easy to give a unified interpretation of the many episodes that gradually did form a path, each having its own weight. The number of players between the Atlantic and the Persian (or Arabian) Gulf is very large, and the political and environmental frameworks equally varied. I hope that the reader understands the reasons for this unavoidable fragmentation, and hope to be able to share my thoughts and impressions. This work first and foremost is about my personal experiences in the field. I consider myself to have been a privileged observer, as it is very rare to have the fortune to enjoy extensive personal autonomy in dealing with governments and important players, as I was able to do in North Africa and the Middle East. Admittedly, dealing with unexpected situations sometimes can lead one to perceive an "exotic" dimension, which may unintentionally receive an overly "literary" treatment in the telling.

The goal of these initiatives was to gradually create a common culture. In other words, to work with the aim that the West and the Arab world might share at least some basic ideas with regard to the great geo-political scenario that surrounds us. In this plan, squaring the circle meant including Israel, an objective that was energetically pursued.

To bring us closer together, serious committed dialogue is required in order to shape what might be called a "common sentiment." In this regard, I can say that some common points of interest were rapidly identified on issues that at the beginning seemed intractable.

A further objective in writing this book was to explain the central role played by the collaboration between the Atlantic Alliance and Arab countries in events such as the war in Libya. It is difficult, though, to fully grasp the continuing influence of events in the years chronicled here (2003-2007).

Finally, the book emphasizes the importance of multilateralism as a methodology, and as the most advanced form of international relations. Today, many international players turn up their nose at multilateralism, preferring exclusive traditional relationships between individual governments. In this way, only each country's national "egotism" is cultivated.

xx

Obviously, it is difficult to make important decisions quickly within the European Union, the United Nations, or NATO. However, negotiation among diverse viewpoints is the best approach for consolidating different interests and values. Even if it is difficult and slow, only in this way can major projects be developed, such as the rapprochement, described here, among highly diverse regions of the world, regions that are in fact already permanently interconnected in other ways.

In the conclusions, I point out that Europeans must believe in themselves, and in their cooperation with the peoples of other world regions, who are pursuing challenging paths. In this way, Europeans also achieve their own interests. This is another way of saying that those who remain absent from the table are always wrong.

To help make this book more comprehensible, I divided it into two parts. It opens with the political situation in the Middle East following September 11, 2001 and the invasion of Iraq. At this time, two parallel initiatives were launched concerning the Mediterranean and the Gulf, and ratified by the summit of NATO's heads of state and government in Istanbul in June 2004. I describe the first exploratory missions to Arab countries in the Mediterranean and the Gulf, and to Israel, highlighting our main objectives in the political-strategic field and the reactions of the countries involved.

The initial political framework was naturally a little confusing on all sides and only gradually became clearer. What emerged was an unexpectedly great interest in dialogue on the part of various governments. There was a growing belief that there was much more in common than initially thought, including with regard to the strategic issues where military and foreign policy intersect.

The second part deals with a series of missions in the region that went beyond the stage of initial approaches and proposed ideas for building a common architecture. This is followed by a number of historical-political analyses that explain how the most important moments of this process are related to current international dynamics.

There are clear differences among the Mediterranean countries, those of the Levant, and those of the Gulf. Then there is Israel and, bordering the Sahara, Mauritania. To better understand events, it is important to view them also in their local context, otherwise it is impossible to understand the overall picture. This section ends with an attempt to draw lessons from past experience for the future and to give an overall view of developments in North Africa and the Middle East.

The book closes with a chapter on the functioning of the international system, multilateralism most especially. This needs to be discussed, because it is so poorly understood among those who are not in some sense experts, and yet is so important for everyone. It is impossible to understand the dynamics of events unless we know how the international bodies of which our countries are members actually work.

An alternative title for this book could have been: "In praise of diversity." Its theme is about finding common values and interests among peoples who have always viewed each other as "different." A tacit optimism runs through these pages; the implicit idea is that it is possible to do unexpected things when there is conviction and a good cause to fight for.

My conclusion at the end of this study is that the best way to advance international governance is by dialogue among and between regions. We can call such "cooperative security" a key factor in tomorrow's world. Why? Without it, the world would be unstable, lacking dominant powers, but with more competition, somewhat akin to an oscillating pendulum. It would be a world with more players than there are today, and one in which it would not be possible for Western values to prevail. This dialogue should be a top priority and tirelessly pursued. The first steps in this direction are described in these pages.

This political journey begun in the Greater Middle East forms part of an evolutionary process underway also in other parts of the world, and should be viewed as such. These historical developments are in the hands of peoples who must make their own choices. This does not diminish, however, the important and positive role that the great democracies can have in accompanying them in these processes, without seeking to dominate them.

PART ONE

A Changing Course for Arab History?

"Do you always travel like this, in planes laid on just for you?",
enquired the Jordanian air force general on welcoming me at Amman military airport. He looked at me with a somewhat surprised
and worried air as I descended the steps of an impressive and cav-
ernous C-130, followed by some assistants. Everyone was fairly
exhausted. We had left Algeria at dawn in heavy rain in order to
arrive on time at 4:00 PM in Jordan. We travelled from west to east
along the southern shores of the Mediterranean, flying over many
centuries of history, perhaps too many for just one trip.

With a forced air of confidence, I replied in an apparently decisive manner: "Yes, of course! Security is always necessary when
travelling!" The general seemed only half-convinced and replied in
a more cheerful tone: "Well! Naturally! I understand that the Atlantic Alliance is important, but normally this plane is used for carrying a company of paratroopers."

Bureaucracy sometimes has procedures that are impossible to
understand. I am sure the C-130 was assigned to me simply because it was the only aircraft available. But, if we had sought to
make an impression, we certainly had succeeded! However this is
not a story about aircraft.

The Atlantic Alliance had never been part of the Middle East's
political framework, which periodically took shape then fell apart
again. The Alliance had been little concerned with the southern
regions of the world, and even less with Arab countries. In all its
publications, NATO wrote that the challenges were to be found
on the plains of Central Europe, from the Rhine to Moscow. At its
headquarters in Evere, in the rainy Belgian capital, the names of all

Russian provinces were known by heart, and there were more than enough specialists and interpreters who knew everything that happened between East Berlin and the Urals.

Together with an air of austerity, there reigned a culture of secrecy, even concerning minor issues. The corridors were plastered with warnings not to discuss confidential matters on the phone. More than once I was tempted to make a collection of them. The terrible coffee was legendary, but became almost a point of pride in that environment permeated by Anglo-American political-military culture, where traditions of frugality and understatement still mattered.

The Fulda Gap, a valley in Thuringia, was the focal point of this culture, a threat that was partly real and partly imaginary. According to the analysts, this was the place where a Soviet invasion of the Federal Republic of Germany, and the world's greatest tank battle, would take place. In Cold War days, the tank was the weapon par excellence. It was calculated that if all the tanks available were put in a line they would cover the length of the Netherlands.

To the south, everything was different. This area seemed of secondary importance, if not irrelevant, during the long years of the Cold War, which we are now forgetting far too quickly. At that time, maps seen hanging on walls at NATO Headquarters ended around Sicily. Indeed the south was viewed simply as a side issue in the 20th-century version of the "Great Game." A metaphorical "here be dragons," that in more recent times has been turned completely upside down. Enough thought is almost never given to how, in recent centuries, only the northern parts of the world have been considered of any consequence, in particular the Anglo-American part. The south was considered a place for travel and adventure, romantic inspiration, lost civilizations, sources of energy, raw materials, and manual labor, and for all that was "other." The countries of the south were not considered real international protagonists, because important world matters were decided elsewhere. Indeed, often in places where there was a very vague idea of what went on in the rest of the world.

True, within the overall context of NATO's post-Cold War outreach, heavily focused on the states of the former Soviet Bloc, the Alliance also had initiated a program of case-by-case contacts with countries in the Mediterranean region, with the stated objective of strengthening regional stability. By November 1995, Egypt, Israel, Jordan, Mauritania, Morocco, and Tunisia had joined the Mediterranean Dialogue, with Algeria joining in 2000.

Frankly speaking, however, this was a low-profile activity, with little energy or political impetus. In fact, when I joined NATO in 2001, I asked the Dean of the North Atlantic Council, i.e. the longest-serving ambassador, for some guidelines on this program, and was advised not to waste too much time on it.

Everything suddenly changed after September 11, 2001. Washington had decided that the new priority for international security was the Islamic world, centered in the southern Mediterranean and around the Persian/Arabian Gulf. The latter generally was called "the Gulf" to make it clear that only one gulf had any real importance. I was a witness to 9/11 and of the speed with which this line was firmly adopted by the United States and the other principal countries, leading to a complete turn-around in priorities. As if it were necessary, a further sign that policies can be the result of unexpected situations.

It seemed in those days that, besides the Twin Towers, the very world itself was collapsing. Lord Robertson, Secretary General of NATO, wanted to make NATO's presence known, but in the first few hours it was not even clear where the attackers had come from. Immense confusion reigned, including fears of follow-on terrorist attacks. Edgar Buckley, Assistant Secretary General for Defense Policy, was the first to write that, if the attacks originated from a foreign country, in other words, an external attack against one of the allies, Article 5 of the NATO Treaty could be invoked, the crucial article that makes an attack against one NATO ally an attack against all.

Initially, the Americans thought this was a step too far. However, they quickly understood that solidarity expressed by the Alliance could carry great political weight and supported the proposal. George Robertson glued himself to the telephone for twenty-four hours, talking to all the NATO heads of government, and obtained their consent to consider the terrorist attacks in the US an act of aggression against which the Allies had to intervene jointly. It was a historic decision for the Alliance and the United States, and made headlines all over the world.

In this context, there was a sudden realization of the great potential a dialogue that brought to the table representatives of Europe, North America, the Arab world, and Israel offered for security. The Arabs were skeptical at first, not knowing how to interpret this sudden interest. Was there something in it for them? Such sudden interest and attention coming from the northern part of the world seemed a little dubious. Western declarations of affection seemed a bit ambiguous to those being courted after years of relative neglect and even exploitation.

Though we should be wary of falling into the trap of imagining that the Arab world is as it is often depicted in literature. I could not help but think of a book that had fired my adolescent imagination. T. E. Lawrence, who had fought alongside the Arab insurgents in World War I against the dying Ottoman Empire wrote: "The [British] Cabinet raised the Arabs to fight for us by definite promises of self-government afterwards ...It was evident from the beginning that if we won the war these promises would be dead paper" (*Seven Pillars of Wisdom*, Introductory Chapter).

In general, Arab governments lacked democratic legitimacy in fragile countries with stagnant economic and political systems controlled by a few people. Across the Arab world, from the Atlantic to the Gulf, material wealth and power were unequally distributed in closed societies. Often the main concern of Arab governments has been to maintain internal stability, rather than to promote the countries' development. Declarations of brotherhood with neighbors have turned out to be contradictory whenever serious problems have arisen.

A classic example is the dispute between Morocco and Algeria (plus the Polisario Front and Mauritania) over the Western Sahara, which the United Nations has been trying to mediate for decades. The land borders between the two biggest countries in the Maghreb remain closed, although UN efforts to promote a negotiated settlement continue.

There is also a chronic dearth of planning in the Arab world. Neither European domination nor that of the Ottoman Empire provided many benefits, and no economically homogeneous area has ever been created. Quotes by famous historians such as Braudel, who spoke of a sea that unites, need to be taken with a grain of salt. For the most part, they are simply literary formulas.

Naturally, political passivity and the weakness of civil society may be explained and justified in a historical context. However, it is wise to remember that for centuries the Mediterranean has been a sea between peoples who still do not know each other well, and with values and interests that are often perceived as divergent.

In part because of such factors, while the trauma of 9/11 and the invocation of Article 5 broadly speaking heightened the focus of the NATO members on threats originating in the Arab countries, and the Arab-Israeli crisis, a contributing factor, was as far as ever from a solution, NATO was still cautious about undertaking any political initiatives vis-à-vis the Arab states. Over decades of laser-like focus on managing, very successfully, the Soviet and Warsaw Pact threat, NATO had become, in effect, a quite conservative organization. It was only in the aftermath of the 2003 Iraq war, which provoked an unprecedented crisis within the Alliance, that a concerted political outreach to the Arab countries (and Israel) would begin.

Fortunately, the Atlantic Alliance as such was not directly involved in the initial Iraq adventure, which nonetheless opened up wounds that despite, every good intention, have not yet completely healed. Nevertheless, every attempt was made to save what could be saved, and to present the outward appearance of shared basic values. The old Atlantic Alliance in those years somehow remained the foundation of that political instrument still proudly called the "Euro-Atlantic community."

The Baghdad Fiasco

There is no denying, however, that, in the rain soaked buildings under the low Belgian sky, which had housed NATO ever since 1967, when Manlio Brosio, then Secretary General, transferred its headquarters from Paris, the political situation in 2003 was far from good. We did not know how to reconnect the strands in the Euro-American relationship, and keeping up appearances was clearly not enough.

Things had started to go wrong at the beginning of the year, when the United States asked for consultations in the Alliance to help a member country facing an external threat. Turkey shares a border with Iraq and the Americans asked for a deployment of forces on Turkish territory to prevent a missile attack. The assumption was that Saddam Hussein was going to launch missiles with bacteriological warheads.

Today all this seems to be outlandish, but it should be remembered that, at the time, the rationale for the war in Iraq was that it possessed weapons of mass destruction. France, Germany, Belgium, and Luxembourg blocked consensus on the US proposal, the French demonstrating the greatest determination. At the level of defense ministers, i.e. without France's participation, since it was still outside the Alliance military structure, NATO ultimately did agree in February 2003 to some measures of support for Turkey. But the political climate had become openly incandescent, something that was in fact quite predictable, given the outcome of a major Alliance exercise a year earlier.

NATO holds an annual Crisis Management Exercise (CMX). Part of military culture, after all, is the cult of maneuvers and exercises. These are carefully planned to deal with imaginary crisis situations. In this way, simulations of what could happen in reality are put into practice. The geo-political background is prepared by experts and is kept secret until the start of the exercise, to simulate real world crises.

In CMX 2002, held from January 31 to February 6, the scenario involved a likely attack against Turkey by a fictitious neighboring country that possessed chemical and biological weapons. Everyone clearly understood that the potential aggressor was in fact Iraq. I don't know how it came to be, but there was a complete absence of common sense in using an exercise scenario of an Iraqi attack on Turkey. The exercise was too uncomfortably close to reality to be considered a purely imaginary scenario.

My role in the exercise was to chair the Council meetings held during the weekend, like during an unexpected crisis. Endless controversies ensued and Onur Öymen, the Turkish Ambassador to NATO, later an important leader of the opposition Republican Party in Ankara, did not know exactly how to react. What could you say about an imaginary Iraqi attack on Turkey using weapons of mass destruction? Would it become a precedent for a real-life situation? Old position papers were fished out, but offered very little guidance. In the end, this impolitic exercise finished in the midst of total disagreement among the allies. They were unable to decide between two options: a preemptive attack with conventional weapons or a threat to respond with force in the event of an attack on Turkey. This presaged the Alliance response a year later.

History books are full of the errors of great nations and, even if his regime was the cruelest in the Middle East, Saddam Hussein was a mistaken target in the post-9/11 political climate. A friend at the RAND Corporation was the first to tell me that Donald Rumsfeld was not satisfied with the CIA intelligence reports. They did not provide proof of the existence of weapons of mass destruction as he had expected. He created a parallel analysis structure at the Pentagon, which gave a very different interpretation to the intelligence received.

What happened later is well known. In the spring of 2003, it only took a few weeks to occupy Iraq, and it was still believed that the Marines would be welcomed with flowers (in part because of the optimism of Iraqi exiles). However, by the end of the year, the political failure of the operation was already evident.

The American proconsul in Baghdad, Paul Bremer, who came from Henry Kissinger's consulting firm and was known for his love of designer athletic shoes, did not think twice about disbanding the army, police, and public administration. He did this without realizing the long-term consequences of his hasty decisions. Bremer was convinced that the regime change would lead the country to a democratic future. Later he wrote that these were not his initiatives, as his orders had come from Washington. Probably he was anticipating what he thought his government would like. In his memoirs, Rumsfeld describes Bremer in no uncertain terms as arrogant and incompetent. It was apparent that, in that circle, there was nobody who had much understanding of the Arabs and regional dynamics.

Although there were some good intentions, there was also great naiveté. The turn of events demonstrates only too clearly that ideology is a bad counselor. In any case, the invasion brought about permanent results by bringing the Shiites to power. Even though they were and remain the majority in Iraq, historically they represented the lower social class. We should not forget that it was the British who in 1920 renamed Mesopotamia, which had no tradition as a distinct, unitary state, as Iraq. In the end, it is certainly a paradox that the events of the last decade have served to harmonize the leaderships of Baghdad and Teheran.

Besides the resources involved, the United States has also paid a high price in terms of credibility. I came to believe that, following the humiliation of the Twin Towers in New York, President Bush wanted to prove he was a leader by showing that he was capable of taking major decisions. In brief, he wanted to show his electorate that he was up to the challenge. He was not totally wrong in saying that it was necessary to work for democracy. It is just a shame he used the wrong methods. A well-known American general, among the many who successively served in Baghdad, told me, for example, that local people were being hired based on the same criteria as those being hired in Pennsylvania, a disturbing thought.

The President received a powerful ideological boost from neo-conservatives, supporters of an imperialistic policy to export values and the free market, and who, for the first time, were very influential in American politics. The neo-cons were convinced that the world was in a historical phase in which it was time for America to rightfully take up the reins of global leadership.

This was certainly not a happy period for American diplomacy. Secretary of State Colin Powell, who had been Chairman of the Joint Chiefs of Staff during the first Gulf War, reluctantly followed the instructions coming from the White House. He suffered from the dominant roles exercised by Vice President Cheney and Secretary of Defense Rumsfeld, who guided defense policy with absolute power.

I saw Rumsfeld at work on several occasions. Once, during a meeting of NATO defense ministers, at a certain point he suddenly asked me how many millions of inhabitants there were in the Ukraine. It seemed to me the sort of thing he should have known, at least roughly.

Later on, in his memoirs, Rumsfeld lamented that Powell did not have the courage to speak clearly with the President. This might well have been true, since it is not easy for a member of the armed forces to change mind-set after leaving a hierarchical world for one so political. I recall, for example, that, at the 2002 NATO-Russia summit held at Pratica di Mare in Italy, the Secretary of State, ever the good soldier, came to tell me that he would have to depart early, as he "had to follow his commander-in-chief," i.e. President Bush. He addressed me because I was chairing the informal lunch of the NATO ministers of foreign affairs plus Russia. At the same time, the Secretary General was chairing the lunch for the heads of state and government.

The United Kingdom was closely tied to the American wagon, perhaps because they believed it would win. This was ultimately a determining factor in Tony Blair's fall from power. Emyr Jones-Perry, the British ambassador in Brussels, advised me to look at the Anglo-American relationship beyond the surface and contingencies. A fine diplomat, he told me that London was fully aware of American "naiveté." However, he also believed that the best option was to remain close to Washington, so as to be able to influence its decisions.

There is a saying, attributed to Winston Churchill, that the Americans take the right decision only after all the other options they have tried have failed. This has happened on a number of past occasions. One only has to think of the two world wars. However, in London they overestimate their influence based on the "special relationship," though this relationship may be cooling, given the new administration in Washington as of January 2017.

During those years, the Arab governments with which I talked listened with one ear, but kept the other out to listen for the noises coming from the Iraqi streets. They were worried that instability there might be transferred to their countries. In private they criticized American errors, but never renounced their relationship with Washington, to which they were tied by many shared interests. In any case, events in Iraq provide crucial background for this book.

New Recipes, But the Same Cooks: George W. Bush's Greater Middle East Initiative

While the United States floundered in the Iraqi sands, in Washington several initiatives were conceived to try to regain the good will of the Arab world. None of these new dishes proved very satisfactory, however, as they were prepared with sauces that went bad, made by the very same cooks who had proved so clumsy in the Iraq occupation.

At the end of 2003, the Greater Middle East Initiative was devised on the shores of the Potomac. It was meant to be approved and supported by the G-7 Heads of State at their 2004 Sea Island Summit, and to be the flip side of the Iraqi coin. It was a wide-ranging action plan aimed at civil society, which would cover the area from Morocco to Pakistan, and was endowed with abundant resources. Its initial weakness was the vagueness of the concept of the Greater Middle East, which called the entire project into question.

Then there were problems of internal coordination within the American administration, and an icy relationship between the Pentagon and the State Department. Attempts by the White House, specifically the National Security Advisor, to arbitrate were not very successful. Overturning normal roles, the Pentagon had the leading role, while diplomacy was forced to reluctantly follow.

The project had a difficult gestation. At the beginning of 2004, the Arab world discovered it, through the leak of an early version of the proposal, published in the London-based Arabic-language newspaper *Al-Hayat,* and rejected the initiative point blank as an attempt to impose Western models. By April, however, the White House circulated a revised version of the plan and US diplomacy was mobilized to make it succeed. This was the product of the strong sense of optimism that characterizes Americans. Several layers were envisaged: political, economic, social, etc. It was meant to show the possibility of radically renewing the Muslim world by promoting democracy, social rebirth and the market. Foreseeing a major deployment of key American institutions, it included foundations, projects for women, and cultural initiatives.

Unfortunately, the basic policy did not function, and there was no public affairs strategy that could fix that. In Brussels, the discussion was heated from the very beginning. The countries that had avoided taking part in the Iraq mission certainly did not want to get their fingers burnt. Those in favor thought they had done enough. The vague definition of the Greater Middle East was a basic weakness and raised questions about the whole project.

That said, a conclusion had to be reached! At a time like this, we could not let the most powerful political-military alliance in history seem inactive. The alliance is transatlantic in its essence and has a long tradition of harmony between the two shores of the ocean. The two NATO secretaries general that I have known, George Robertson, a British Labourite, and Jaap de Hoop Scheffer, a Dutch Christian Democrat, are both representatives of the generation for whom being a good European meant being convinced of the centrality of the transatlantic relationship. A policy that benefited everybody for a long time.

An opinion emerged that it was necessary to do something to respond to American appeals, and at the same time address common concerns about these new challenges. It seemed possible to approach the Arab world on matters such as security and defense, those vitally important areas where foreign policy, questions of strategy, and military action intersect. In the end, the Americans gave up the idea of trying to deal with the entire Islamic world. They had to admit that countries from Morocco to Central Asia were too diverse to be lumped together.

Given that it is a geographically homogenous area, we at NATO became convinced that it was possible to open a dialogue with the Gulf region, central to American interests but also of primary importance for Europe. Therefore, there was a common interest in drawing it closer to the Western world. This included six countries

(Saudi Arabia, Kuwait, the United Arab Emirates, Qatar, Bahrain, and Oman) that already had a degree of organization in the form of the Gulf Cooperation Council.

The American ambassador to NATO was the young and ambitious Nicholas Burns, first spokesman for Secretary of State Madeleine Albright, then ambassador to Greece before taking up his NATO posting, and ultimately Under Secretary for Political Affairs under Secretary of State Condoleezza Rice (2005-2008). A man of great talent, who wanted to succeed. He had a difficult job, and when he spoke at the North Atlantic Council, he always stayed in line with his instructions. The administration he represented was at the apex of its power and few sought to argue with it openly. One exception, though, was the French representative, Benoît d'Aboville, a shrewd professional, who in turn had his own instructions to carry out.

It should be noted that the United States has often been criticized. It is easy, however, to turn up one's nose when others are assuming responsibility. Not everyone knows to what degree most countries around the world turn to Washington for support on issues that actually are of no concern to the Americans, and in which they absolutely have no desire to be involved.

The Flight of the Phoenix

In the debate about NATO outreach described in the previous chapter, the European side raised a question of principle. They were in agreement with the US on cooperation with the Gulf countries, but believed that it was not possible to ignore the traditional ties that existed with the southern shores of the Mediterranean, i.e. the Maghreb, Egypt, etc. It would have been illogical and counterproductive to do this, precisely when a new policy towards the region was being launched. The European governments insisted on this point. In other words, it was not possible to ask the Alliance to support new ambitious initiatives towards the Arab world while neglecting the Mediterranean. They had to run in parallel with the rest of Middle East.

Also, healing the wounds of transatlantic controversy would take some time. Following his 2004 re-election, in March 2005 President Bush made a trip to Europe to seek to reinforce ties with the Allies. In fact, given the very divergent positions, a complete rapprochement still was not actually possible. Nevertheless, all the correct rituals of friendship were performed in the temples of the Brussels institutions, including the European Union. Masking differences with formalities and good manners does help to heal wounds. During the week of the visit, the *Economist* had an amusing cover showing Bush the explorer in a dugout canoe making his way through the jungle – Europe – full of pitfalls, traps and snakes. We were all talking about it.

Colin Powell had visited the North Atlantic Council in April 2003 to show proof that Saddam Hussein had weapons of mass destruction, and that he maintained relations with terrorists. He brought with him, to support this theory, some fragments of intelligence that no one, including himself, knew how to evaluate, judging from how he later distanced himself from them. The presentation was an unfortunate event, as Powell had always conducted himself in a dignified manner.

In any case, NATO was being dragged into the international relations crises of the moment, and in this political context the Secretary of State proposed a meeting of Alliance ministers of foreign affairs. The main item on the agenda was the much anticipated discussion on political-military and strategic relations with the Arab world. The meeting was held on April 2, 2004 in the form of a private working lunch at NATO Headquarters. The poor dining quality there was legendary, almost raised to the level of branding for NATO. At a certain point, the Secretary General finally decided that enough was enough, and since then a catering service is used whenever there is a ministerial meeting!

Despite, or perhaps because of, the poor food, the right decision actually was made. In a compromise, everyone agreed to elevate the relations existing largely on paper with seven Mediterranean Dialogue countries to the status of a "Partnership," of course with the advance approval of the governments in question. It was also agreed that the six countries of the Gulf Cooperation Council would be contacted, to seek their approval for the launching of a parallel dialogue.

The discussion at the April 2 foreign ministers meeting was not heated, thanks in part to the extensive preparatory work the permanent representatives had carried out. Important differences, however, had emerged during that phase. Broadly speaking, the US pushed hard for an initiative, especially vis-à-vis the Gulf countries, while the European allies were split. Some, like Italy, were open to the initiative, while France, in particular, was opposed. Ultimately, France and some others agreed, seemingly in part because they seemed to believe not much would come of it.

The summit of NATO heads of state and government scheduled for June 2004 would put the final touches on this agreement at the highest political level. Istanbul, straddling Europe and Asia, and the nearest NATO capital to the Middle East, seemed the ideal location to launch this new initiative, which NATO now viewed as an historic event.

In hindsight, it may seem surprising that, given its vocation for crisis management, the Euro-Atlantic community was caught flat-footed by the realization of how important the Arab world was, with all of its ramifications for international security. Fundamentally it was 9/11 that most dramatically changed the Alliance's outlook. For NATO, the countries of Islam had once again become key historical players, and the tanks of the Cold War era, now visibly useless, have been placed in mothballs.

Clearly, it had taken some time for this to sink in. For example, after the fall of the Berlin Wall and the dissolution of the Soviet Union, there might well have been political repercussions in the Middle East. Instead, nothing happened in the short term. A fire was smoldering beneath the ashes in the Middle East, but it took another twenty years before it fully rose to the surface, when the people of several Arab countries rose up to challenge the inadequacies of the regimes in power. Like the Phoenix, the sacred bird of ancient mythology, which symbolized rebirth and whose flight was the harbinger of a new and important period. We do not know whether the future of the Middle East will be positive but it will certainly be important.

Finally on the Road South

With Euro-American harmony on the mend, at least, and general satisfaction with the launch of NATO's Middle East initiative, it was time to shift from guiding principles to concrete action. For example, how make the right moves to draw closer to these peoples who were so important, but also seemed politically and psychologically distant? The dimensions of this challenge had not yet been identified, but, as always, when governments make difficult choices they want to see immediate results.

The first objective was to have a closer relationship with the governments involved, and convince them to participate by presenting our proposals in the best light. This was essential, because relations with Arab countries historically had been strained because of a lack of prior consultation. This created an understandable discontent. In the past, it had been easy for the Arabs to claim that initiatives originating from the West were "one-way" and what they thought was considered secondary. Since things were changing at the speed of light, we wanted to show that the lesson had been learned and to behave with more respect.

The Istanbul Summit was scheduled for June 2004, just two months after agreement had been reached in Brussels. An important political event like this had to be carefully prepared, to ensure that everything would go right. Unlike those of the European Union, NATO summits are not "routine" events, held at fixed intervals, but are decided on as needed.

The Council asked me to conduct a round of consultations in the capitals involved in the initiative, and to write an urgent report on the results. It was risky to use the prestige of the Secretary General (de Hoop Scheffer had succeeded Lord Robertson) in a project full of uncertainties, which could easily fail. Therefore, it seemed better to send me, the Deputy Secretary General, his number two.

In any case, no high-level representative of the Alliance had ever been to an Arab country. There was a complete absence of any tradition of mutual understanding and good neighborliness. Instead, stereotypes abounded on both sides. In Brussels, there were still many questions concerning the Arabs' willingness to establish a collaborative relationship. Negative reactions were certainly possible.

Therefore, I found myself with a mission that had to be concluded in haste, and conquer a challenge in unknown territory. It is never easy to transform a political directive, which is necessarily schematic, into a detailed operational plan. Whoever gets the job has to be quick about it. Then there is the problem of timing, how to do things and where to begin. It was not easy to get from one capital to the other seven. It was easier to return to Europe each time and then set off again. This, however, would take too much time.

It would have been far better to have a plane at my disposal, but how could this be done? The tradition was that only the Secretary General was entitled to ask for one for trips abroad. Fortunately, the Italian Delegation at the North Atlantic Council convinced the Italian Prime Minister's Office that it would be positive for the national image if I presented myself in the capitals with visible backing.

For political as well as logistical reasons, I decided to go first to the Mediterranean and then visit the Gulf, and to begin with Morocco and then proceed eastwards along the coast. Logically, my ideal counterparts would be the ministers of foreign affairs of the various governments and, if at all possible, the ministers of defense or the chiefs of staff of the armed forces. Our minimum objective was to meet at least one top government member in each country, to whom I could present our proposals, highlighting the main points and recording their official reactions. Given our tight schedule, this was no easy task. The government leaders with whom we hoped to meet might well have other commitments, be out of the country, or simply find an excuse for not meeting with me.

Unfortunately, it was quite clear that the Mediterranean Dialogue process, initiated in 1994, had not resulted in significant links, with operational significance, that could facilitate this new Alliance initiative. Since NATO itself did not have embassies in the places we were to visit, we had to prepare everything from Brussels by phone, fax or email. Neither could I rely on the national diplomatic structure of a member country, not wanting to choose one rather than another. Also, I did not want to start off on the wrong foot by giving my Arab counterparts the impression that I was being remotely controlled by any particular Alliance government. The relationship between the International Staff (IS) and member countries is always a delicate matter in NATO, with governments tending to limit areas of competence. On the other hand, the IS attempts to avoid interference by national governments.

Not being able to organize everything in advance, once I arrived in a capital, I would have to finalize the meeting schedule for the following day in the next country. We had to organize everything at the last minute, relying on NATO's standing. During those years, the Alliance was a symbol of success, given its leadership in the Cold War, and was highly respected. We also arrived on the heels of successful operations in the Balkans, and represented a very strong transatlantic relationship. Today, following the difficulties of the Afghan campaign and the weakening of historic relations with the US, the case is perhaps different.

Protocol dictated that we spend at least one night in each country. Anything less would have been considered rude. It was not possible to remain in an Arab capital for just a few hours. In my case, however, I could not stay more than one night because otherwise I would not have been able to return to Brussels in time to present my report.

I proceeded with this series of consultations relying for the most part on luck. Certainly not the idea an outside observer might have about a prestigious international organization, but that is the reality in which we work. I was accompanied by a representative of the Secretary General's Private Office, a Political Affairs representative, one from Public Diplomacy, a colonel from the International Military Staff, and a security guard.

In hindsight, I was lucky, even if right from the beginning there were a number of strange events. For example, departing for Rabat from Melbroek military airport, we initially were unable to find the plane that was to have been sent from Rome. Finally, an Italian Air Force Piaggio materialized on the runway. It was the smallest plane I had ever seen. It could only carry a maximum of eight passengers, with the luggage stowed in the gaps between the seats. It certainly did not look like a plane carrying a high level international delegation on an official visit.

We had to reroute in order to refuel, and a few hours later found ourselves sitting in the midst of local technicians and workers at the airport cafeteria in Alicante, in southern Spain. As fate would have it, we finally landed in Rabat a few hours late, and were welcomed by the Chief of Protocol from the Ministry of Foreign Affairs, who was unable to conceal his shock at the arrival of his official guest on such a seemingly inadequate aircraft. He made a few ironic comments, comparing the long distance the plane had covered with its small size. I learned that, in situations like this, which happen now and again when travelling around the world, it is best to put up a good front. I tried to display the calm indifference of someone who is used to travelling in all kinds of transport.

These hardships were immediately forgotten after an unexpectedly positive meeting with Minister of Foreign Affairs Fassi Fihri Tahib. It was clearly appreciated that, for the first time, a high-level representative of the Alliance from Brussels had been sent to consult with the Kingdom of Morocco. This experience was repeated several times in other capitals, highlighting the importance of direct personal relationships. "Telephone diplomacy", so much in use in our times, is a tool that does not convince anyone. In passing, the Minister made a point of telling me that told me he was familiar with the Venice Biennale art exhibition, as his wife was an artist.

I was told that Morocco had a more ambitious foreign policy than would appear at first glance, and that it was heavily invested in the Atlantic and African dimensions. The world seen from Rabat was full of grey zones, where the Alliance could create a good position for itself. Although Morocco publicly was taking a cautious stance, a much more positive attitude was evident during talks with the top officials, who generally had a broader vision. In the background, there was also the fact that Rabat had a moderate attitude towards Israel, the result of the age-old presence of an influential Jewish community in the country.

Morocco believed that its political position had much in common with that of the Western world. It ran the risk of destabilization due to extremism and terrorism, as well as being exposed to every sort of trafficking that originated in Africa. Being located at such a difficult crossroads, Morocco seemed to want a better relationship with the Alliance, which was attempting to be friendlier to the Muslim world. This was understandable, given NATO's political importance and its historical character.

Another conclusion was that our relationship should improve on its own merits, and not allow the Israeli-Palestinian conflict to take it hostage. The Minister expressed his concern, however, regarding enlargement of our partnership to the Gulf countries. This quite surprised me. He said that Morocco was well aware of the stability problems and other difficulties in the Gulf, but Mediterranean issues were profoundly different. In conclusion, he feared that we would no longer have enough resources if the initiative were expanded to encompass the Arabian Peninsula.

Immediately afterwards, there was a meeting with the local press in the lobby of the Foreign Ministry. Initially I was somewhat anxious about how to explain the Western Alliance in an Arab capital. My way out was to say that we wanted to provide added value to, but not replace, the relations that already existed between Morocco and other countries. In fact, no new organizational bodies, councils, etc. were being planned. Had that been the case, we would have spent more time discussing procedures than talking about substantive issues.

This was the best guarantee of good faith and mutual benefit. At the beginning of each year, a list would be drawn up of joint actions to be carried out, and would be periodically updated. In short, so as not to create problems for our hosts, I highlighted the positive reactions of the Moroccan government without characterizing them as a change in policy. I was surprised by the apparent naiveté of the media questions and the respectful manner of the journalists present, who were not yet hardened like their crafty European colleagues. But perhaps this was due in part to the unfamiliarity of the subject matter.

The day's political accord was sealed that evening, in a traditional Arab villa transformed into an elegant guesthouse, where we were guests of Secretary General of the Ministry of Foreign Affairs Youssef Amrani. He, like the Minister, was a member of the emerging upper middle class that was slowly leading the country towards a society in step with the times.

King Mohammed VI of Morocco was one of the first Arab leaders to respond to popular requests for reform. He introduced important innovations, delegating greater authority to the government, declared Berber an official language alongside Arabic, and improved popular representation in governance. This was visible in the elections held at the end of 2011. In other words, he is one of the few Arab heads of state who has sought to get out in front of events, instead of suffering their consequences.

During long journeys along the southern shores of the Mediterranean, I in fact came to the conclusion that the Maghreb had significant affinities to the European countries along the sea's northern shore. If led in a gradualist and wise manner, it seemed liked it could, within a generation, become the embryo of a Euro-Mediterranean community. Despite the challenging events of more recent years, I still believe the Maghreb should be a priority in European policies.

I immediately lost the good mood I was in when I found out that the plane that was supposed to take me to Algiers the following morning was no longer available. I had an appointment at 11:00 A.M. with the Minister of Foreign Affairs in the Algerian capital! Late that night, I was told that a large C-130 transport was on its way from Pisa. Normally, this sturdy aircraft is used to carry helicopters or a company of paratroopers. It would be landing in Casablanca, a few hundred kilometers away, because the runway at Rabat was too short. This change in plans meant getting up at dawn, but we arrived in Casablanca only to discover that regulations required that the pilots rest for another seven hours.

My French assistant Thomas Wagner, however, rightly convinced me to continue the trip to Algeria, which I had already decided to cancel, by pointing out that the people with whom we were to speak would not want the meetings cancelled, and would adjust their schedules.

We ended up leaving many hours late, very stressed and worried about not honoring our commitments. Not only was it raining, it was cold. Because it was neither designed nor built primarily to carry passengers comfortably, a C-130 has no frills, not even heat.

Algeria is of top strategic importance, and its stability is in the general interest. It is biggest country in the Maghreb, and supplies a large part of the energy consumed in Europe, especially Italy. It was only slightly affected by the events of the so-called Arab Spring, perhaps because it had withstood years of Islamist insurrection and well understood the impact of terrorism. A difficult country, in some ways still finding itself after the brutal war for independence from France.

We finally arrived in Algiers in the driving rain, cold, and not knowing what kind of welcome to expect. Receiving high-ranking NATO representatives was a novelty, which probably explains why we also were met by the German ambassador to Algeria, our NATO-country point of contact for the visit. The Algerian officials seemed astonished to see me arrive in such a massive aircraft that was clearly for military use. Once again, I was asked some tongue in cheek questions about how I normally travelled.

This was an opportunity to appreciate Arab flexibility. First, I was told that the Minister of Foreign Affairs had rearranged his schedule to accommodate my arrival. This meant I would have to spend the night in the capital, before continuing my journey the following morning to Amman. I certainly could not refuse the offer, the price of which, however, was another dawn departure, since the captain of the C-130 had warned me that it would be a good eight-hour flight to reach Jordan from Algiers.

Foreign Minister Abdelaziz Belkhadem, then in his sixties, was a veteran from the ranks of the National Liberation Front (NLF) that had led the struggle against French domination that came to an end in 1962. Since then, the NLF's historic leadership has taken turns holding the reins of government, while younger people have remained waiting in the wings. This seemed to confirm one of the frequent accusations against the country's governing class, namely the absence of any change at the top.

The office in which he received me was Spartan, so unlike the elegant offices typical of many ministries of foreign affairs. However, he proved to be much more positive about a policy of collaboration than I ever would have expected, given the lack of historic precedents. It seemed that Algiers welcomed the opportunities offered by this unexpected initiative to accelerate a process, already quietly under way, of drawing closer to the West. President of the Republic Abdelaziz Bouteflika, in fact, subsequently visited NATO's headquarters not once, but twice.

Behind the official facade, the main problem was the relationship with Israel. Here there was no tradition, like in Morocco, of Arab-Jewish comity. In Algeria, the Jewish community was completely identified with French domination. Therefore, it followed that any hint of publicity that gave public opinion the impression of a policy of collaboration with Jerusalem was to be avoided.

Except for this issue, however, the Minister made it clear that he was very much in favor of having a serious relationship with the Alliance, even going so far as to propose a "Mediterranean Council" and a protocol of cooperation to be updated every year. Algeria was positive concerning the fight against terrorism, as well as NATO's scientific program. Nevertheless, Belkhadem, like his colleague in Rabat the previous day, maintained that Algerian needs were too different from those of the Gulf states for them to be together in the same group.

In Algeria, the priority was to strengthen security in the Mediterranean, and he insisted that we concentrate on that issue. An inter-ministerial committee already had been established to coordinate relations with the Atlantic Alliance, including both the military and civilian sectors. Our meeting with them was interesting. At least at first glance, their administrative system appeared to resemble that of France.

One of the main issues was Algeria's participation in Active Endeavour, a NATO Mediterranean naval operation to prevent terrorist activity, launched after September 11. We invited them to take part in the operation, as this would have increased its overall symbolic value. On the other hand, I understood that there was some hesitation from a political standpoint to link the government so directly to a Western anti-terrorist operation.

Alongside Minister Belkhadem, I had a press conference to explain the new climate and the content of this common initiative. Like in Rabat, it was easy to handle by Western standards. It was in itself positive that the local authorities publicized the event, even if the journalists did not appear to be very up to date on major strategic issues.

I gathered that the frontier with Morocco was still closed, an indication that Arab brotherhood, though a much-celebrated principle, often was not put into practice. The former Spanish Sahara was still contested by the two countries, and Algeria did not acknowledge Morocco's sovereignty over the region. At the United Nations, they had been racking their brains for years to resolve this question, proposing compromise solutions that had been rejected by one party or the other.

Multilateral diplomacy is different from traditional diplomacy, and requires the sometimes-difficult compliance of multiple, diverse actors. That evening a dinner was organized at my hotel, to which the German Ambassador also was invited. He seemed pleased and interested in participating in this unusual event. As often happens in southern countries, around the table an unexpected discussion developed concerning the destiny of the world and our roles in it. At that point, everything immediately became very informal. The representatives from the ministries of foreign affairs and defense made some arguments about issues of long-established relevance to NATO that were not terribly sophisticated, but had the uncommon virtues of freshness and sincerity.

Every time I have discussed politics in informal settings such as this, I have been struck by the Arabs' sense of frustration, which immediately comes to the surface. They feel they are left on the margins in world decisions and considered second class countries. There is a certain sentiment of vindictiveness directed towards America, but also towards Europe. They criticize the West for its hypocrisy and double standards, for asking without giving, and for excluding participation. Reference to the Israeli-Palestinian crisis is inevitable, an open wound and humiliation that crops up as soon as polite formalities end.

Algeria is a big country that would like to replace Egypt as the main Arab country of the Mediterranean region. Its main difficulty lies in having a very young population, frustrated by the lack of opportunity, and a governing class that belongs to another generation. Also, sooner or later it will be necessary to make great investments in the infrastructure and to incorporate the Sahara. That day, however, has not yet arrived.

Although the city's urban structure is clearly European, that evening I was surprised how modest the hotels were in Algiers, a capital that evidently has remained off the tourist track. I was put up at the historic hotel where Eisenhower and other heads of state had stayed. Even though it was the middle of spring, my room was cold, and it was difficult to turn on the lights. However, it was by no means an unpleasant experience. Perhaps it was more honest in a developing country, compared to the grand anonymous international chain hotels spread throughout the Gulf.

After the excitement of such a long day, I could not wait to get to bed, especially knowing that I would have be awake just a few hours later, since Algiers airport was going to be opened for me at four o'clock in the morning, again in the rain, as it turned out. I was worried that I was getting sick, but managed to get going and maintain a dignified appearance. This type of diplomacy requires not only a sound nerves, but also the health of an ox.

I once again boarded the C-130, which was beginning to feel like home. Under the compassionate eyes of the crew, I tried to summon up the usual optimism, despite our weary eyes and bedraggled clothing. As the pilot once again reminded me, that plane was not designed to carry passengers. We took off for Amman, which was certainly not around the corner, but due east near the other end of the Mediterranean.

What could we do to pass the time? Work? Read? Look outside? Sleep deprived, and given the C-130's lack of comforts, we quickly decided to abandon any pretense of rank or formality and wrapped ourselves up in our coats and tried to sleep on the rough canvas seats on either side of the aircraft. Lying there, I began to wonder whether I would be able to carry out this demanding mission in a satisfactory manner.

From the Maghreb to the Levant

Crossing the Mediterranean, you fly over regions with historic, well-known names, yet vastly different in terms of physical appearance and of society. After the Arab conquest and conversion to Islam, a divide was created between the north and south of the sea, which saw the Crusades, piracy, the rise and fall of the Ottoman Empire, and colonial domination. Only now are we beginning to reflect seriously on how to bring our societies closer together. We are beginning to see the mutual benefits in such an interconnected world. This is a hard task, given the misunderstandings that have occurred over time, and is an open challenge at the highest level.

As we left the Maghreb behind us, making our way eastwards, the landscape became increasingly arid. I caught a glimpse of Leptis Magna in today's Libya, birthplace of Septimius Severus, the only Roman emperor of African origin, and other great Roman cities of the late imperial era. Their yellow stone columns were shining beside the eternal blue of the sunlit Mediterranean. The region is rich with civilizations that disappeared centuries ago, but were at the time unequalled in their development and physical harmony. Today they appear out of place, enveloped and submerged in the desert sand. On leaving Egypt, one enters the Levant, another region with ancient civilizations and a long history.

It may seem strange, but the political order in the Middle East is still based on agreements made between the United Kingdom and France after the First World War, but also rooted in wartime events such as the 1916 Sykes-Picot agreement, dividing up spheres of influence, and the 1917 Balfour Declaration regarding a Jewish state. The nations of Jordan, Syria, Lebanon, Iraq, Israel (formerly

Palestine) and Saudi Arabia all have their origins in the post-World War I settlement.

Before leaving for my trip, I had studied the birth of the Hashemite Kingdom in Jordan, which deserves a mention. In 1921, following his appointment as Colonial Secretary, the first thing that Winston Churchill did was to visit Cairo. Before boarding his ship, he received a note from his staff suggesting that he "establish a political system in Trans-Jordan which was different from the one in Palestine, one centralized under an Arab ruler acceptable to His Majesty's government."

During the trip, Churchill met Emir Abdullah, son of Sharif Hussein bin Ali of the Hashemite dynasty, which had fought against the Ottoman Empire alongside the British Empire. Churchill convinced him to accept the throne of a country whose borders were still being drawn in pencil on the maps of Arabian desert.

Finally, we arrived within sight of Amman, which stands in the middle of a rocky desert, with an important history. Jordan has some large Roman cities, as well as historic Petra. A Jordanian Air Force general was there to receive us, and once again there was a quick exchange of jokes: "Is this how you always travel? On a plane this big, just for you? Amazing, what a way to do things!" My host believed the Atlantic Alliance wanted to impress their interlocutors by flaunting its means of transport. He could never have imagined that it was due to planning problems in the Italian Prime Minister's office, and had nothing to do with an established policy. In fact, the logistical problems continued, but obviously I could not complain in public and was required to exhibit a certain amount of authority.

It was immediately apparent that the Jordanian infrastructure was superior to anything I had seen in North Africa. Amman's military airport looked modern and efficient, as did the planes that could be seen in the hangars. Entering the city, there were newly-built hotels on well-maintained roads, dignified government buildings, and orderly traffic.

That day I had a meeting with Minister of Foreign Affairs Marwan Mouasher, a member of the country's Christian minority, indeed the only Christian I met on my travels in the Middle East. We met in his tastefully furnished office, which was elegant and understated in style. He projected the image that Jordan wanted to present, that of a moderate and open country. At present, he is Vice President for Studies at the Carnegie Endowment for International Peace, and he coined the popular expression "Arab reawakening."

Bordering on Israel, Saudi Arabia, and Syria, Jordan's position is difficult, both geographically and politically. Following the 1948 war (after the declaration of the State of Israel) and their resulting exodus, plus population movements after Jordan lost the West Bank in the 1967 war, Palestinians account for sixty per cent of the population.

Therefore, the questions raised by the Minister concerning the scope of Alliance initiatives in the civil and military areas were well justified. He asked many questions concerning the connection between the Mediterranean Dialogue and the initiative for the Gulf. Jordan is located right in between these two areas, something the Minister pointed out in no uncertain terms.

From his point of view, every political move had to be within the context of the Arab-Israeli conflict, giving it priority over all other issues. Given the difficult atmosphere, the real question was how you could include Israel in a multilateral political forum, ignoring the main problem. I had to provide a complete description of the scope of our intent, which was above all to build concrete ties, but without trying to tackle the main problem, which in any case we were unable to solve.

Another thing that worried the Jordanian government was the proliferation of international diplomatic initiatives in the region, some of which were not very persuasive. Where were we with respect to the American Greater Middle East Initiative? In fact, he had a point. In speaking with him it was clear that Jordan was a central point with respect to unresolved Middle Eastern issues.

Jordan is the only country in the region that enjoys good relations with all its neighbors, including the dynasties of the Gulf. Basically, the King has an ably conducted, balanced policy that is respected because the reasons for it are clearly understood. Beyond standard diplomatic relations, there is also an unpublicized direct line between the Hashemite dynasty and Jerusalem. The good relations that the royal family has wisely managed to maintain around the country are highly useful, as Jordan has no natural resources and does not produce a drop of oil. As we have seen, the country was born of unusual political circumstances.

I had the opportunity to meet King Abdullah in Brussels. His perfect English accent and the character of his opinions seemed to come from another part of the world. His sister Princess Aisha is a professional military officer, with paratrooper's wings, now holding the rank of major general, who graduated from the UK military academy at Sandhurst, from Oxford, and from the National Defense University in Washington. She has advised the US Department of Defense on integration of women into the armed forces, and has represented Jordan on the NATO Task Group that deals with the psychological, organizational, and cultural dimensions of terrorism. I had the pleasure of meeting her in Brussels in 2005, where she spoke to me at length about the importance of promoting the participation of Jordanian women in the armed forces, an effort that had the King's full support.

It does not take long to realize, in fact, that the armed forces are the true power base for the continuing rule of the Hashemite dynasty. The King, himself a former officer in the army, takes a personal interest in its daily management. As further proof of this link, when I asked to meet the minister of defense, I found out that there was none, as that position is held by the King. In other words, he is the direct superior of the chairman of the Joint Chiefs of Staff, for whom personal relations with the royal family are thus a daily duty.

Considered the best in the Middle East, the Jordanian Armed Forces are well trained and equipped, and often train abroad. Apart from considerable American assistance, there is also a tradition of strong ties to the UK. Let us not forget the legendary Arab Legion, commanded by an English general who was re-named Glubb Pasha.

As he had come straight from field exercises, the Chairman of the Joint Chiefs of Staff was in camouflage. In excellent English, he told me he approved without hesitation a political relationship with the Atlantic Alliance and more concrete cooperation. We had to find the means to achieve it, he added, giving the impression that he did not have any specific ideas on this. My conclusion was that it was vital to give these initiatives practical content.

It was clear that Amman was a natural point of reference for the whole region. In the hotel elevator, I met a group who someone told me were Iranians. Staring at my unmistakably Western jacket and tie, they commented among themselves while giving me cold looks of disapproval.

At the end of my stay, I called the Norwegian ambassador, who was our NATO-country point of contact in Jordan. He did not seem to be very much in the know about NATO matters, and was happy to get a long briefing.

The next stop was Jerusalem, and I decided to travel by land, rather than by plane, after having received the blessing of the authorities of the two countries. My border crossing had to be dealt with at the highest levels, and no one was there who did not have authorization.

The distance between the two capitals is minimal. It is an interesting experience to travel from Jordan to Israel driving by the Dead Sea and crossing the historic Allenby bridge. You can reflect on how much or how little you know about the land's ancient and modern history. I could not help but look around, from the Dead Sea to the cultivated countryside, which bore no trace of industrialization. The officer accompanying me indicated that it was the wealthiest part of the country which otherwise was quite dry and barren.

General Allenby, for whom the bridge is named, commanded the British forces in the region during World War I, when the Ottoman Empire was nearing its end. T. E. Lawrence wrote: "[Allenby] sketched to me his next intentions. Historic Palestine was his, and the broken Turks, in the hills, expected a slackening of the pursuit. Not at all!" The General then outlined his plans to push on toward Amman and Damascus. (*Seven Pillars of Wisdom*, Chapter 113).

This old iron bridge is highly symbolic, a small link that can create the illusion, indeed the hope, that something more solid could be built, transforming it into a highway.

The Jordanian colonel who was accompanying me mentioned that the Jordan River, the border with Israel, was guarded by two divisions, the bulk of Jordan's army. On both sides of the bridge, the border posts have a designated liaison officer, whose identity is made known to the other side. The two communicate on a special dedicated line.

While I was enjoying a coffee in a gracious atmosphere at the border post, I was surprised by the arrival of a long black limousine. It had come from the Israeli side, and a tall official in a dark suit, sporting a white shirt and yarmulke, got out. The suit, by its cut, was unmistakably American. He was a young man with a strong Brooklyn accent, who cordially welcomed us and told us we would now be setting off for Jerusalem.

I could not resist the temptation of asking where he came from. He confirmed that he had been born in New York, where his parents still lived, and had emigrated a few years earlier, before entering the Israeli diplomatic service. His physical appearance was so typically American that it was somewhat shocking.

Crossing into Israeli territory, Nicola De Santis (who ably took care of public diplomacy with the Middle East for NATO) informed me that Egyptian Minister of Foreign Affairs Ahmad Maher had just announced to the press that he did not think my visit to Cairo useful "as Egypt [did] not believe that NATO [had] any role to play in the region's political, economic, and social reform processes." This was another example of how crucial the problem of perception is in such a complex region. Egypt had misunderstood the purpose of my trip as an attempt to convince them to accept the content of the Greater Middle East Initiative. This was by no means the first time this kind of misunderstanding had surfaced.

On the trip to Jerusalem, surprisingly short for those unfamiliar with the local geography, we passed by Jericho, as well as other places whose names are well-known, not only for their biblical connection, but also for their importance today. By actually getting to see the local geography, I realized that the Middle East crisis plays out in an area that is small, but where every square meter of territory seems to be of infinite worth. No other region in the world has produced proportionately as much history, philosophy, people, and politics of importance for the outside world.

These thoughts made me forget my lack of sleep, tiredness, and tension regarding the task ahead. The walls of Jericho passed before my eyes, high on a hill, under a clear sky and burning sun. Laden with enormous diversity, tension, and on-going history, Jerusalem dazzled me. Aside from Rome, it is perhaps the only place in the world that sums up so much of human civilization. Anyone who does not see Jerusalem is missing something.

The King David Hotel, often used for official business, is bursting with charm and history, and slightly retro with a colonial touch. So many people have passed through this hotel. Just the view of the old city and the golden domed mosque is worth the trip. This is what I was thinking as I looked toward the horizon, where everything contained centuries of history.

In the course of a few hours, many meetings took place. First, I met with the Secretary General of the Ministry of Foreign Affairs and with Ministry of Defense representatives, who tried to evaluate whether Brussels seriously intended to raise the level of relations in the Middle East, and whether there was any potential comparative advantage for Israel. The approach was very different from that of the Arab countries. The conversation was rather more complex, for one thing, because Israel has an active partnership with Washington, highly trained and equipped Armed Forces, an excellent intelligence service, and seemingly a better knowledge base for understanding NATO's perspectives.

Even though we were not known interlocutors, I got the impression that Jerusalem saw the advantages of participation in a wider network of political contacts, and not just focusing on bilateral relations with the US. Moreover, the Mediterranean Dialogue was the only inclusive and non-discriminatory mechanism for regional collaboration in the political and security field, since it offered all participants the same opportunity for cooperation, whether Arab or Israeli. The Dialogue also would provide the possibility for consultations with Europeans and North Americans with little publicity. This had important political significance for Israel, but was also tacitly understood by the Arabs. Perhaps it was the major added value of the whole multilateral cooperation exercise we were trying to put into motion. In the end, my counterparts expressed their interest and complete availability. MFA Secretary General Ambassador Yoav Biran added "the more the better" when referring to NATO/Israel cooperation, and expressed his opinion that Israel could profit from it.

The next day I went to Tel Aviv to meet General Ziv, chief of operations, also with responsibility for the Gaza Strip. The hills drop rapidly as you leave Jerusalem heading toward the Mediterranean, which, again, is surprisingly close. Travelling at high speed along the highway, I remembered one of Amos Oz's novels, in which he tells of how his parents lived in Jerusalem, but how he also had cousins in Tel Aviv, all having come from Eastern Europe. Before the Second World War, there was only one telephone line linking the two cities, and the families called each other once a week to see how everyone was doing. There was the sensation of a huge physical divide, and this telephone line was truly essential. Today we can find this amusing, while looking at the skyscrapers and fashionable restaurants along the shores of the Mediterranean. A further surprise comes when you realize how close all this is to Gaza.

I found the general very sad. He told me that, just the day before, a jeep carrying five young soldiers on patrol in the Gaza strip had been blown up by a land mine. He was in the middle of negotiating with Hamas for the return of their remains. Being a true soldier, he spoke frankly, saying that a solution could never be achieved by military means alone. He said with conviction that sooner or later a political agreement would have to be found with the Arabs.

On leaving his office, I had a horrible feeling of impotence, that things would drag on for goodness knew how long, with no one able to put an end to such a waste of human life. What was striking for any visitor to Israel was to see as many women as men in uniform, a clear demonstration that the Israeli Defense Forces are a people's army and that everyone has the obligation to defend their country.

All around the bustle of daily life was in full swing. The sight of Tel Aviv with its lively beach life bursting with places of entertainment was very striking. This all seemed very far away from the complications of internal Israeli politics, marked by fierce opposition parties and coalition governments that never enjoy an easy life.

While we were on our way to the airport that evening, the MFA official from Brooklyn talked quite openly about this. He maintained that the religious parties represented a modest minority of the electorate, however the right and left were so equally balanced that the minority religious parties often ended up with their fingers on the scale.

We arrived at the protocol lounge. I have seen many such rooms all over the world. This one was small and slightly messy, different from the somewhat anonymous and functional ones in Europe, the luxurious ones in the Gulf, or the humble but still dignified ones in the Maghreb. The personnel represented the amazing diversity of Israel, home to people from all the four corners of the earth, each bringing with them their own distinctive history.

It had been planned prior to our departure that Egypt would be included on this trip. What had happened? In Cairo they apparently did not know how to take the Atlantic Alliance initiative, and were afraid of compromising themselves.

The Egyptian ambassador in Brussels, Soliman Awaad, afterwards diplomatic advisor to President Mubarak, told me that a visit to Cairo was premature and that there had not been enough preparation. Minister of Foreign Affairs Ahmed Maher also telephoned NATO Secretary General de Hoop Scheffer and politely told him that, at that time, the political situation in the region was very serious, and any new initiative might be badly interpreted. In spring 2004, receiving a mission from the Alliance from one day to the next might have been a step too far. NATO was a symbol linked too closely to the West, the US, and military issues. In sum, we had to put off any engagement with Cairo until the right moment.

In Mubarak's time, foreign policy reflected a delicate internal equilibrium. Since the Nasser's day, the government has had a non-aligned vocation. However, Egypt recognizes the State of Israel and receives sizeable economic and military aid from the United States, on which it depends for survival.

Egypt is unique in the world. Overpopulated, the area of the country that can be cultivated extends just a few kilometers on either side of the Nile. This is a daily miracle that Egyptians have had to live with forever. It is no exaggeration to say that, if this great river ever dried up, the country would disappear.

Importantly, though, with its universities and respected institutions, Egypt is considered the mother of the Arab world. There is also a sizeable Coptic Christian minority, descendants of the ancient Egyptians.

From the Mediterranean to the Sahara

At last, the aircraft we were waiting for arrived to take us to the next destination, Tunis. With the prevailing winds blowing from west to east, i.e. against us, it took over four hours to reach the Tunisian capital in the middle of the night. I soon was installed in a huge apartment at the Sheraton. It was a characteristic of those years to find myself in rooms that were far too large for the number of occupants, and sometimes only for stays of a few hours.

Tunis is the most European-looking city in North Africa. It is relatively prosperous, and has a modern urban structure, with visible traces of the important Italian, French and Jewish communities who have lived there for generations.

Tunisia is a traditionally moderate country, having known how to reap political fruits by becoming the seat of the African Development Bank. It has maintained excellent relations with France, its former colonial power. Revisiting the country over the years, I had the impression that it was the only non-oil producing country in the region that had undergone a slow but steady process of development.

Still, in December 2010, the spark that set fire to the region was precisely in Tunisia, a protest against food shortages. This outburst was visible proof of the inadequacy of the Ben Ali regime.

In fact, the wave of popular demonstrations that spread as far as Oman was a reaction to deep-rooted problems that, although not visible on the surface, had been present for some time. These problems were so submerged, however, that France made the blunder of proposing assistance in policing just a few days before the dictator Ben Ali hastily fled to Saudi Arabia. Fortunately for Tunisia, like in any relatively developed civil society, there was no tradition of military intervention.

At 8:00 AM I met with Foreign Minister Habib Ben Yahia, a veteran of many government posts. I had already met him when he was the minister of defense, when I was on a bilateral visit to Tunis with Italian defense minister Andreatta, for whom I served as diplomatic advisor.

With great courtesy, Ben Yahia, a man of the world, explained that he knew about the Mediterranean Dialogue, as he had taken part in its initial launch, and that its reinforcement proposed in the NATO initiative was a natural follow-on. That sounded encouraging. He emphasized that, given his position in the government, he considered everything from a political viewpoint, and said explicitly that curbing extremism and terrorism seemed to him to be common concerns for the West and for Arab countries.

I was no longer surprised by my hosts' warm welcomes for NATO's openings to the region, for which I was the spokesman. Nevertheless, I was aware that the positive response and encouragement of governments differed from the mood in the streets, where there breathed a general mistrust toward the West in its various forms, without making distinctions. This means that even Europeans are not loved, both for the colonial past and for the suspicious attitude towards Islam held by large sectors of European public opinion. The episodes concerning cartoons of the Prophet Mohammed published in the Danish newspaper *Jyllands-Posten*, and in the French satirical weekly *Charlie Hebdo*, as we have seen, have left deep marks in the entire Muslim world, from North Africa to Indonesia.

There is also a historical fascination with conspiracy theories. Things are not taken at face value, but rather are seen in terms of the behind the scenes interests of the powerful. Some even claim that the attacks on the Twin Towers in New York were concocted by the US administration to justify the war on terror.

Another thing that is clear is how Arab societies are top-down, with little representation from civil society. Tunisia was the first embark on the path of change, and in time we will see how far the reforms will go. Despite threats and other difficulties, Tunisia so far seems to have had better luck than the other countries touched by the Arab Spring.

Encouraged by Ben Yahia's words and warm welcome, I left the Ministry accompanied by the Chief of Protocol. Being a protocol officer, passing the years meeting people, often only for a few hours or minutes, is a job that never interested me. Yet in every diplomatic service there are those who love it, an example of the diversity that can be cultivated in the international professions.

Minister of Defense Dali Jazi showed that he was very well informed and was clearly positive towards developing relations in the military field. He even indicated that he did not rule out participation in future missions, provided they were under a UN mandate. He emphasized in particular the exchange of information and professional training.

It almost seemed as if a memo had been circulated, since here, like in the other capitals, they wanted to focus attention on the Mediterranean. The Tunisians too feared that the initiative would be diluted by the inclusion of Gulf countries, which they perceived as distant in terms of common interests, and perhaps also in terms of values. I often asked myself whether this was a matter of principle or they actually thought that resources would have been diverted away from the Maghreb.

Tunis was the only capital where we touched upon the issue of relations with Libya. The starting point was that the Libyan regime was unpredictable and a potential source of instability. However, the ministers added that, at the time, positive developments were underway in Tripoli, and the Tunisian government had good relations with Qaddafi, encouraging and supporting his gradual return to the international community. (Of course, the comprehensible optimism of 2004 would be dashed some years later.) In conclusion, the Tunisians extended their good offices for the possible inclusion of Libya in the Mediterranean Dialogue. An idea which, to be honest, I already had been considering, and that, at the time, offered some positive aspects. I had discreetly consulted the US ambassador to NATO on this question, but he answered that such an initiative was premature, given that the United States did not, as yet, have diplomatic relations with Tripoli. (Full diplomatic relations were restored in 2006.)

Mauritania

I was attempting to clamber over some desert dunes in Mauritania, to try and immerse myself more fully in that unusual reality, when the phone rang. At the other end of the line was the ambassador of the Gulf Cooperation Council in Brussels. He proposed a meeting for the next day with the foreign minister of Bahrain, who was on a visit to Europe. The phone connection was perfect, and he was astonished when I explained that I actually was in the West African desert, but would be happy to go to the appointment. This was one of Mauritania's many contradictions: although remote, its telecommunication service was more than adequate.

My program had been organized in a way that left only a Sunday to visit the Mauritanian capital, the furthest stop of my trip, deep in the desert on the border with Senegal. This meant I had to cross all of the Tunisian and Algerian Sahara. The Mauritanians initially resisted this somewhat high-handed approach to organizing the visit, even if it was dictated by necessity. However, in the end, Nouakchott was not really able to pressure an organization like NATO. Thomas Wagner had ably conducted the negotiations. A suitable compromise was found. The Minister of Defense would receive me, but at his home, not in the office.

Here I need to make a geo-political digression to explain why Mauritania would participate in the Mediterranean Dialogue. Although this country is located partially south of the Sahara, it is also part of the Maghreb, and a member of the Arab League.

The government was enthusiastically supportive of political-military cooperation with NATO. I have never really completely understood why, since it is difficult to imagine the world as seen from Nouakchott. What are the challenges they fear? Who are their enemies, and who are their friends? I think they considered us to be protectors of the country's integrity, helping them against terrorism, as well as arms and drug trafficking.

Flying over the desert between Tunis and the sand dunes bordering the Atlantic, the view from the plane was quite different from what we had been used to. After a long flight across the Sahara, an urban center appeared in the middle of the desert. An unattractive, random-looking arrangement, with sheet metal roofs and ill-defined roads.

With trepidation, our small group prepared to face the airport in front of us. We were very pleasantly surprised, however, by the friendliness with which we were greeted by the Chief of Protocol and the senior officials who accompanied him. Certainly, it was a colorful group. The styles of dress included military uniforms, white robes, turbans, and double-breasted pinstripe suits with heavy bracelets. The influence of nearby Senegal was clearly evident.

The Chief of Protocol promptly announced that the President wanted to meet me on Monday morning at eight, just before my departure for Brussels, an offer I could hardly refuse. An immediate meeting with the Minister of Defense was on the schedule. Our motorcade proceeded through dusty streets in the midst of huts, sad looking markets, and alongside buildings under construction that tailed off into the desert. When I close my eyes, I can still see that scene. In a modest-looking neighborhood, we stopped in front of the house of Minister Ahmad Ould Sidi. He received us in the living room, with officials seated on either side of him. He only said a few words, while the Navy Chief of Staff spoke at length about the friendly presence of NATO ships in Mauritanian ports, which, to be honest, I had never heard about.

In Mauritania as elsewhere, it was my job to propose a partnership project of far-reaching political and military cooperation, with profound geopolitical implications. As we spoke, it was clear that our hosts were having difficulties. Their horizons did not extend much beyond neighboring countries. Because of his difficulty in dealing with the subject, at one point I even began to wonder whether the person in front of me actually was the defense minister. In any case, the Mauritanian response was very positive and I had done what I had been sent to do.

The best hotel in the capital was a modest Novotel with a small swimming pool. We were invited to a dinner, and the thing I remember best is the Mauritanians' continuous use of mobile phones, which I quickly realized were considered very important accessories. There were all kinds of them. Some were sparkly, others emitted intermittent flashes of light. My service issue phone was being eyed with disdain and I was asked candidly why a powerful organization like NATO would make do with such modest equipment.

In the meantime, I was preparing myself mentally for my meeting the next morning with the President. The Presidential Palace is an unattractive cube-shaped building. Before being ushered into the presence of the head of state, we walked through a series of empty audience rooms with gilded chairs all lined up against the walls, according to Arab custom. Finally, we found ourselves in front of a man with an imposing moustache, who had taken power in a coup, twenty years earlier, and who in the future would be deposed in the same way, while on a trip to Saudi Arabia.

President Maaouya Ould Sid'Ahmed Taya gave a complicated speech on the importance of globalization, all of which seemed somewhat remote when viewed from that palace. He then asked in no uncertain terms to be invited to the NATO Istanbul Summit. Being unsure of what meaning to draw from this conversation, I threw in that, as the daughter of the Italian ambassador to Senegal, also accredited to Mauritania, my wife had attended the Mauritanian independence celebrations. I diplomatically omitted the fact that the Mauritanian minister of foreign affairs had lavished undue attention on the ambassador's daughters.

The President formally invited me to visit the country with my whole family, for a tour of the Mauritania's beautiful sites. I accepted, glossing over the matter of the invitation to Istanbul, which seemed completely unrealistic.

On leaving the meeting, I met local media representatives, who introduced themselves with an almost obsequious air. It appeared that the journalists' job was to highlight the international role of their political leader, rather than providing the public with information. Indeed, when leaving the corridors of power in developing countries, you often are left with the impression that main objective of the heads of state is to maintain internal control for themselves and their clans.

For Mauritania, the question is also how to get out of the tunnel of underdevelopment. There are oil and gas reserves off the Atlantic coast, but the country is unable to develop them alone, and therefore must entrust them to foreign companies that have their own interests, which are certainly not the same as local interests. I was taken to the coast to see the fishing port. With its simple wooden boats, it was a picturesque place, pulsing with humanity of great dignity dressed in colorful robes. It was truly a life lesson.

Since I had a full day ahead of me, my hosts suggested an excursion into the desert. "Saints and philosophers are those who like to live in the desert", said the Secretary General of the Ministry for Foreign Affairs with a smile. In fact, the desert makes up most of the country, and is its main feature. A desert worthy of a film, with sand somewhere between pink and yellow. There were natural dunes formed by the wind, on which I was able to walk barefoot toward an endless horizon that every so often was broken by the presence of shrubs and a few bare trees. Nature seemed to be seeking revenge for man's pretensions. The sparse vegetation was full of thorns, and offered no shade from the sun. What a leap from the familiar lush green shores of the Mediterranean.

Our guides told us that it was usual to travel to Niger and Mali by camel caravan, routes also taken by terrorists and drug traffickers. But the attractive exotic dimension of this human horizon allowed us to imagine a world we believed had already disappeared.

At this point in our consultations, contrary to the pessimism at its outset, I began to think that the mission was proving to be a success. Using the right tone, it was possible to engage the Arabs and, despite many problems, identify areas where our interests converged. It seemed the approach we had chosen was basically spot-on: prior consultations, concrete proposals, emphasis on individual, national preferences, promoting the multilateral approach as complementary, and a practical two-way street. With a new store of knowledge and excitement, we headed back to Europe, but only after the usual wait for the plane, always a different model, that never seemed to arrive from Rome.

If I think back to my experiences of those years, a pattern of a certain obsession with planes emerges. I have seen all kinds with many different owners. This was not a completely mindless fixation because the possibility of getting things done in good time depended largely on the means of transport.

As there were no NATO embassies or offices abroad, whenever I arrived in a country I had to rely directly on the local government, forcing me to deal with all kinds of protocol offices and security services.

We made our way across deserts and the sea, back to rainy Brussels, where there was absolutely nothing new. At the end of demanding missions, you may well feel tired, a little excited, and enjoy a sense of freedom that is an instinctive reaction to having overcome a challenge. However, this psychological state never lasts long. You get involved with something new, another problem to deal with, a new challenge.

In fact, having just landed in Brussels, I had to quickly prepare my report for the North Atlantic Council explaining the political meaning of the reactions of the governments we had consulted, and propose the way ahead. In this task, Alberto Bin of the International Secretariat Staff was invaluable.

How to Learn to be Together

The report prepared after my consultations provided, I think, a relatively clear overall picture of the situation. I was well aware that my report would shape how member states decided to follow up in the dialogue. I thought about this as I looked out my office window at the flags of the NATO countries fluttering wildly in the wind.

I had written that, along the southern shores of the Mediterranean and in Israel, the governments consulted had no objection to entering a real partnership along the lines that had been proposed. I proposed a plan for periodic programs both for military aspects and the wider field of security. These were essentially practical projects, designed not to duplicate what already existed, but, as had been clearly pointed out to everyone, to provided added value based on the expertise of the Alliance and its member countries. Consultations on political issues would take place primarily at the bilateral level, during periodic meetings at the level of ambassadors, ministers of foreign affairs, and defense ministers. These consultations were to include Israel.

In all of my contacts, I had emphasized the principles of "sharing" and "the two-way street." In other words, there could no longer be unilateral decisions, where the Arabs found themselves facing positions taken without their having been previously consulted. This is something the great powers had always done in the past, in this way offending the sensibilities of others. With the experience I had gained, I had come to understand that this aspect was of great symbolic significance, and that respecting these principles was much appreciated.

Arab bureaucracies are generally not very proactive on the

practical level. This is not only due to systemic difficulties, but also because they are not used to working with Westerners in fluid and operational ways. In brief, we were facing a situation of limited ability for concrete planning, but great attention to form, a lot of sensitivity about presentation and how to negotiate, which Western interlocutors generally did not take sufficiently into account. Therefore, in order for the message to be well received, it was opportune to continue to emphasize sharing and "non-imposition."

I concluded my report by underscoring that a great international organization that was made up of the most advanced countries in North America and Western Europe could offer a range of opportunities that was superior to that of traditional bilateral relations, but that the methodology would be the decisive factor for success.

I remember that the North Atlantic Council's informal discussion of the report, in preparation for the following day's formal meeting of the Council, was held at the rather austere Spanish embassy. I had opted to write in a very direct and clear style, perhaps not very diplomatic, and to make straightforwardly positive recommendations based on my meetings. The report was received, in fact, with a certain amount of surprise. I received some questions about the responses of individual governments, and the feedback was all quite positive. US Permanent Representative Nick Burns, voicing what many had said in private, said that he had expected a cool reception for the initiative and was expecting a report with multiple caveats. Clearly, events in Iraq also were weighing on him, and he seemed relieved that the outreach effort, which the US had pressed for, appeared to be on track.

It seemed, nonetheless, that some of those present had difficulty understanding that the situation was now very different, because it was going in the direction of common interests and mutual defense. It promised cooperation and assistance in sensitive areas where the recipient countries had real needs, which went hand in hand with guarantees of sharing in decisions. As we know, even for very qualified professionals, it is sometimes beyond anyone's abilities to conduct wide-ranging, outside the box analyses. Every government tends to see the world through their own national logic, and automatically advance their own interests, or what they think is in their interest.

At the end of the discussion I received unanimous approval for this unexpected success and the new prospects that had been opened up. There was just one objection, on the part of Spanish Ambassador Juan Prat y Coll, because, when I was in Morocco, I had failed to inform his embassy, which was supposed to be my contact point. If he had known the complicated circumstances of that eventful mission, he would have saved his breath.

The Council decided to prepare a policy document to present to the Arab governments and Israel for their approval, before its official adoption at the Istanbul Summit of the heads of state and government at the end of June 2004. The Council also decided to proceed with a round of visits to the Gulf countries as quickly as possible.

New Friends in the Gulf

I have to confess that, after so much tension, the idea of setting off again on an equally tiring and difficult trip to unfamiliar countries held no attraction for me whatsoever. However, sometimes luck unexpectedly intervenes. I learned that, the very next week, a meeting of the ministers of foreign affairs from the European Union and Gulf Cooperation Council countries was to be held in Brussels.

So there was a chance of meeting with these Arab leaders without having to make the trip to their capitals. I could hardly believe my good luck. Another fortuitous coincidence was that almost all the ministers would be staying at the Hotel Conrad, the largest in the Belgian capital, and generally also the most popular with Arab dignitaries, as it was similar to luxury hotels in their own countries. I knew a number of Arab ambassadors who had resided at the Conrad for long periods upon first arriving in Brussels. While staying there, they were able to conduct unhurried negotiations with the owners of rental properties, who were determined to capitalize on their luck that Belgium's relatively small, provincial capital city had become a major international center.

In addition, back at home there were the unfathomable bureaucracies of their capitals. The Ambassador of Qatar, the young and friendly Sheikh Meshalh Al-Thani, for example, explained to me that the furniture for his residence had been chosen and bought in Doha. This involved all sorts of problems, not the least incompatibilities of style between the furniture and its intended setting.

However, at that moment, my problem was much more substantive. I was waiting with trepidation for responses to my requests for meetings. What should I say to the ministers I was going to meet, and, more importantly, how was I going to say it? Taking into account that we were dealing with unfamiliar countries, what were the right arguments to promote the initiative? As there were no precedents, it was essential to start off on the right foot.

One afternoon in May 2004, I was admitted to the suite of Prince Saud Al-Faisal, Minister of Foreign Affairs of the Kingdom of Saudi Arabia, or simply "The Kingdom," as it is often called. The Prince was the dean of the foreign ministers of the entire world, having held the post since time immemorial. This, in itself, was an important message. Together with some colleagues and protocol officials, I waited patiently for his arrival.

 He was a rather pleasant interlocutor. Handsome, tall, aristocratic, with impeccable manners, he belonged to the inner circle within the royal family, which gave him undisputed authority. He was the competent and noble face of the dynasty.

I realized that, in his eyes, I represented an organization worthy of respect, when he apologized three times for being twenty minutes late, blaming the traffic in the Belgian capital. He explained that he had just come from New York, and was leaving the next day for London. Tea was immediately served in small cups without handles, as is the Arab custom when offering tea to guests.

I told him that the purpose of our meeting was in part to explain the historical development of the Atlantic Alliance. It had come a long way, was reinventing itself and undergoing a profound transformation. NATO's evolution meant there would be partnerships with significant countries with shared political and military interests.

I explained that we wanted to establish a wider international security network to contribute to global stability, to consult on the political agenda, and establish military cooperation without duplicating what was already being done by Saudi Arabia on a bilateral basis. Interoperability, border security, the fight against terrorism, proliferation of weapons of mass destruction, reforms in national defense systems, and information exchange all seemed natural areas of common interest. Hence our proposal to establish stable relations with the Gulf Cooperation Council countries, which in time could become a true alliance.

Prince Saud did not seem at all surprised, and reacted with

courtesy and attention. After a series of comments about the international situation, he said that NATO's development seemed to be in line with current trends and the overall international framework. He found nothing wrong with an approach that could be beneficial to his country and the region. He agreed that it was necessary to find innovative formulas to better ensure international security, and that the Atlantic Alliance had a reputation for seriousness and a history of success, such as in the Balkan crisis, as well as the Cold War.

Clearly, he was not in a position to give a definitive answer right away, which seemed logical. He concluded by saying he understood the importance of this proposal and would put it before the King and the government on his return to Riyadh. The fact that he accepted the logic of the proposal and wanted to take it further was in itself a positive sign. We should not forget that Saudi Arabia is by far the most important country in the region and can exert its influence on neighboring countries.

The next day I continued my diplomatic "tour" with the foreign minister of Kuwait, Sabah Al Salim Al Sabah, of Bahrain, Muhammad bin Mubarak al Khalifa, and of the United Arab Emirates, Sheikh Abdullah Al-Nahyan, meeting them in their suites or in meeting rooms of the Hotel Conrad. My interlocutors appeared satisfied with the steps taken so far, and seemed interested in my presentation, which I adjusted according my impressions of them and their countries' interests. These gentlemen were a very diverse group. Some were in traditional Arab dress, while others looked very Western. The ministers of Bahrain and Kuwait were members of their respective royal families.

I tried hard to give precise answers to their questions, to give them the impression that these meetings had been well prepared on a personalized basis. Some asked if there were any connections with the situation in Iraq. There were none, because the Alliance had no combatant role in that country, and limited itself to operating a small training mission from 2004 to 2011.

Kuwait and Bahrain were the most enthusiastic, perhaps seeing an opportunity in dealing with an organization with so much experience. The fight against terrorism was indicated as a priority, along with regional stability, the management of Iranian claims etc. The initial reaction of each and every one was that the proposals were interesting, both on a political and military level, and that they would therefore give a complete and full report to their respective governments.

Oman and Qatar were not represented by ministers of foreign affairs, but rather by secretaries of state. They too were interested, which bode well for our future relations. The Omani representative was the most surprised, being an outsider in the Brussels international circuit, as Oman did not have an embassy in Belgium.

The conversations ended with assurances that we would share in advance all documents to be sent for approval at the June NATO Summit in Istanbul, a process parallel to that for the Mediterranean area. This was an opportunity to emphasize once again the importance of the "two-way street" to the Arab world. It might seem only a diplomatic nicety, but it was not. We made a commitment to no longer consider this part of the world to be on the receiving end of decisions taken in Western capitals, but as partners with whom to travel the road together. The Arab world is so important that we must accept its reality, despite the challenges and contradictions, in order to move forward together.

Was it the winds of Middle East history driving NATO, which, after winning the Cold War, was looking for new challenges on the shores of unfamiliar seas? If it were not for the tragedy of September 11, would any of this have ever happened? Until recently, Western interest in the peoples of the Arabian deserts had been rather narrowly focused on oil and gas and the need to keep them flowing. The concept of multifaceted and multilateral partnerships with these countries was new.

On my first trip to Qatar, I was told that, in the past, the water shortage had been so bad that the inhabitants were used to drinking slightly brackish water, without suffering any consequences to their health. I also remembered a story told by Amedeo Guillet, an Italian ambassador and war hero, who had spent a long time in that part of the world. In his usual entertaining way, he explained that air conditioning was a recent conquest.

He told us that, in the early 1950s, when he was posted to Saudi Arabia, the US ambassador in Riyadh was the only one to have an air-conditioned room, which actually was his bedroom. When he had dinner guests, he used to reward them with a guided tour of his residence, which would end up in that very room. Things change, of course, and brackish drinking water and the absence of air conditioning are now things of the past, forgotten in the maze of skyscrapers, luxury hotels, and supermarkets kept at polar temperatures that grace the region's capitals today.

The Istanbul Summit
NATO's Political Leaders at Work

None of the permanent representatives to the North Atlantic Council really went into the details of my second report, on the meetings with the Gulf countries, before approving it. They knew too little about this new front, but perhaps also felt that the initiative had now acquired its own momentum, due to the earlier decisions at the foreign minister and permanent representative levels. The Alliance's decision-making bodies did what they were expected to do, agreeing on the texts of two "declarations." One concerned the Mediterranean Dialogue, and the other was entitled the "Istanbul Cooperation Initiative." Still today, these are seen as good examples of political dialogue and cooperation in the political-military field.

These declarations clearly expressed the will to strengthen international security and enhance regional stability. They listed concrete areas for cooperation that ranged from countering weapons of mass destruction, the fight against terrorism, and border controls to the reform of defense systems and so on. To meet our commitment to prior consultation, we circulated the proposed texts of the declarations to the ambassadors of the Mediterranean and Gulf countries in Brussels. No one made any negative comments.

The package was therefore approved in Istanbul on June 28, 2004, in the presence of the heads of state and government of the NATO countries. Everyone there reaffirmed their strong political interest in North Africa and the Middle East. The Americans were happy because the Gulf was treated as a priority area, the Europeans because they had gotten attention for the Mediterranean, and the Arabs because their concerns had been acknowledged.

Like memories, over time documents tend to fade. Few people now recall the Istanbul Summit as a historic step for the international community. At the time, however, it seemed as if we were launching something really significant on an important front. Laymen cannot imagine how much time and energy is spent on policy documents that need to be agreed down to the last comma, especially in a consensus-based organization like NATO, where any member can wield veto power. Despite the challenges, I had the feeling I was working effectively, in a good cause.

I remember the Summit as a highly colorful event, to which distant countries, such as Afghanistan and the republics of Central Asia had been invited. President Bush announced that American control over Iraq would end two days earlier than planned, transferring authority to the Iraqi government on June 28 instead of June 30. This announcement, however, had very little effect on the audience.

Among the European political leaders present was Prime Minister Manuel Barroso of Portugal, not yet President of the European Commission. President Jacques Chirac of France acted as if he were at home, constantly chewing peanuts and tossing the documents that he had finished reading over his shoulder without looking. The French Minister of Foreign Affairs Michel Barnier and Defense Minister Michèle Alliot-Marie picked up these sheets of paper like schoolchildren following behind their teacher.

Scandalized, NATO Secretary General Jaap de Hoop Scheffer told me that German Chancellor Gerhard Schröder was annoyed by the length of the official dinner, because he was unable to watch his favorite soccer team play in the German championship.

Afghanistan's President Karzai circulated wearing the traditional karakul hat and multi-colored robe that have made him famous. As always in an elegant blue suit, President Bush gave a side speech in which he expressed hope for Turkey's entry into the European Union. a subject about which he clearly knew very little. Finally, there was a big concert at Topkapi, the historic palace of the Ottoman sultans, which overlooks the Bosphorus and has a magnificent view of the Asian side of the city.

I have attended several of these summits, where the international community tries to put its best face forward. They are showcases for host governments, but also opportunities to give a more human face to important international actors by seeing them up close.

The Challenge of Putting
Political Commitments into Practice

After a delicate round of consultations and presentations, the agreement on target countries and the initiative's underlying principles had been signed. It was now necessary to move on to the next phase. That meant creating an architecture for which only the political foundations were in place. Clearly, this was going to have to be dealt with in several stages.

As we have seen, these initiatives were the result of a political compromise. It would have been different if the United States or Europe had decided to go it alone in reaching out to the Mediterranean or Gulf countries. Although far from perfect, these multilateral initiatives represented an important step forward.

We can see immediately that, in the world, there are few active contributors to collective security and the general equilibrium. There are many more "security consumers." i.e. countries that export problems, or remain passive, with little interest in what goes on around them. There is clear interest in increasing the number of governments willing to take on responsibility, countries that strive to improve the stability of the world in which we all live. Naturally, each contributes according to its means.

The creation of the network described in these pages was the first concrete experiment towards this goal, and will probably be the way of the future. In Libya in 2011, Arab countries tried for the first time to become producers of security in this sense, by contributing to the fall of Qaddafi. It was a noteworthy initiative, even though the Libyan intervention has had unanticipated negative consequences.

Of course, we must keep in mind that, not only is there still a long way to go, but that at the start there were virtually no relationships, and there was even hostility. As mentioned before, our priorities were to open a political dialogue, reform the defense sector, have military interoperability, and contribute to the fight against international terrorism. Basically, to look at problems together and initiate projects where there was added value, without the pretension of being the exclusive players. Political dialogue also includes the exchange of confidential information, a practice that has only just begun and requires mutual trust. In such a critical region, an extensive and deep political-military "network" would make a positive contribution to world security and stability.

Among the areas of NATO's special expertise is the reform of national defense systems, something that even its critics acknowledge, for the simple reason that NATO has done it for decades for its members and aspiring members. At the forefront of these reforms are the democratic control of the armed forces, budget transparency, and public access to information. These are the most obvious. But there are others to which less attention is given: the reduction of military personnel, their reintegration into society, relations between civilians and the military, and, of course, training.

"Cooperative security" is a new approach to global stability that complements the work of other organizations such as the EU and the UN. Each country can decide what they need; there is flexibility as to the type of relationship, and each country's specificity is taken into account. Naturally, this is a long-term process that can succeed only if there is continuity.

On the basis of a shared political assessment, additional countries can be included. It seemed for a time, for example, that Libya might be included, though those hopes were dashed.

Our first work program was designed to prevent the need for experts to negotiate principles every time. This was another way to avoid confusion created by national bureaucracies. The number of activities offered to Mediterranean Dialogue partners, for example, grew rapidly, from 100 in 2004 to more than 700 by 2011.

We tried to establish a relationship whose watchwords were "increase stability" and "project security." It is a bumpy road that leads to collective security on an equal footing. Both personnel exchange and working on joint projects is vital. This is easy to say, but certainly hard to do. Above all, when dealing with the countries of the Alliance, it is necessary to maneuver carefully to obtain their consent. Political agendas were and are divided. For example, Spain sees the world differently from Lithuania.

Our Mediterranean and Gulf interlocutors were different and not used to being together. There were controversies missed by outsiders, but that became manifest when you got down to the details. The most delicate aspect turned out to be inclusivity. These offers of cooperation and assistance were to be open to all, without discrimination. But it was clear, just to mention two extreme examples, that countries like Mauritania and Israel were very different and that the more developed countries could reap the greatest benefits.

Diverging perceptions and objectives, of course, are not restricted to NATO's cooperation with the Mediterranean and Gulf countries. An interesting episode concerning the general principles of world governance involved Croatia. Between 2005 and 2008, its government was considering holding a referendum on NATO membership. There was little enthusiasm, though, except for the thought of joining a "club" that was considered exclusive.

The Croatian ambassador in Brussels, Milutinović, convinced us that we needed to be seen more often in Croatia. I was sent to Zagreb, where I met with Prime Minister Ivo Sanader. Our conversation began with a tedious exposition of the efforts made by Croatia to improve its defense capabilities and to increase its contribution to operations in Afghanistan. Minister of Foreign Affairs Kolinda Grabar-Kitarović and the Minister of Defense added further details.

Kolinda is noe President of Croatia, and I have maintained good contacts over the years. I do not really know why, but at a certain point I had to intervene. I thanked Sanader for his presentation, but pointed out that, in my view, his primary interest in NATO membership should be different and of greater relevance. By entering the Alliance, Croatia would be changing its international status. It was no longer a government to which decisions taken elsewhere were announced. There was no longer the need to go and gather information in the great capitals. The country would have a place at the table with the principal democracies and participate in decisions on major issues. This was a quantum leap forward, and a new way of thinking was needed. Sanader, an interesting man of Dalmatian origin with some knowledge of Italian, responded by saying that he fully agreed, and had not previously seen things in this way. He instructed the ministers to take note, and invited me to speak at the University of Zagreb and to the media. This exchange highlights the significance of participation in international responsibilities. Today, a greater share in world governance is in everyone's interest, even for a small country.

I had occasion to re-read the text of a press conference I gave in Kuwait in September 2007 to the KUNA national press agency and the newspaper *Al Khaleej*. The text read: "Today globalization has erased forever the idea of being safe because of geographical distance. Increasingly, the security of nations is put into question by events taking place elsewhere." There is only one way to respond to this state of affairs, and that is to go beyond traditional geographic, cultural, and religious boundaries to explore new avenues.

This type of opening and active participation has to be the Atlantic Alliance's brand for the twenty-first century. First and foremost, human minds must interact and share knowledge to create conditions for cooperation and security. It is quite possible to have reservations as to how high a priority these principles should be given, but the goals seem to me to be ones that could be easily shared.

A Weekend in the Gulf Region

The challenge remained, however, how to put the promises of Istanbul into concrete practice with our new friends. Kuwaiti Ambassador Abdulaziz Al-Sharik, who was particularly active, often came to visit me in Brussels to express his hope for closer ties in the future. He also told me a surprising story. His fellow citizens who were abroad during Saddam Hussein's occupation of Kuwait lived on the dividends of a national fund that prudently had been placed in a London bank years earlier. This illustrated the Kuwaiti sense, at that time, of being in a precarious situation.

In September 2004, I landed in the Kuwaiti capital starting there the first visit to the Gulf, curious about this new world of which I knew nothing. Over time, I discovered that the country's society was relatively more developed than that of its neighbors. It is ruled by a historic royal family, the Al-Sabahs. In 1897 Kuwait became a province of the Ottoman Empire. In 1913, it became a British protectorate in order to block the planned railway from Berlin to Baghdad, the idea of the Kaiser and the Young Turk government. In fact, because of World War I the railway was never built.

For all these reasons, Kuwait had greater contact with the rest of the world than its neighbors. Today, by regional standards, it has more than decent institutions, universities, and newspapers published in English. The veil did not seem to be obligatory, and I ran into women holding official positions.

Kuwait certainly is not responsible for its choice of neighbors, occupying a thorny position. Fronting on the Persian Gulf, Kuwait is close to the Shatt-al-Arab, the contested border between Iraq and Iran.

I had arrived at a very delicate moment: Iraq, the invader in the 90s, was experiencing bloody upheavals on the Kuwaiti border, where powerful Shiite factions were fighting each other. Also, the Sunnis had lost the power they traditionally had held, and the principle of "one man one vote" now made them a minority. Naturally, the Sunnis were in revolt against the new Shiite-dominated government, which explains in part the virtual breakup of Iraq, and the consequent situation of insecurity and instability in Kuwait's immediate vicinity.

I was put up in an enormous hotel suite in the antique French style, with a mini bar filled with drinks in various attractive bright colors, none of which were alcoholic. At first glance, Kuwait City was not an historic capital, crisscrossed by wide streets lined with ordinary-looking modern buildings. It was, however, the anteroom of a world different from the one we were used to in the Mediterranean, where centuries of regular communication and interaction along and between the shores had created a certain knowledge and acceptance of each other's habits. In the Gulf region, on the other hand, a model of modernity was superimposed on tribal peoples who had had limited interaction outside the area.

I wanted to understand what the Kuwaiti leadership thought about security, and its attitude towards its difficult neighbors. My first dilemma was how to introduce myself, and the character and tone of my conversations with the Kuwaitis. I thought about this while riding through the semi-barren streets of the capital, preceded and followed by large dark SUVs that unceremoniously blocked the traffic as we passed. Clearly drivers were accustomed to giving precedence to important visitors and respected police authority. The athletic-looking men who were with me did not seem to be in the mood for joking.

I found it unusual that the minister responsible for the security services was in charge of coordinating our visit. I later discovered that Vice President of the National Security Bureau Sheikh Thamer Al-Sabah, whom the Emir had designated as the liaison with NATO, was in fact a very kind and hospitable person, and a friend. I remember one occasion when, at a certain point, he said that he had to end our conversation because he could not arrive late for a family dinner. Thamer Al-Sabah is also a cultivated and very professional man, now President of the Bureau.

My first meeting was with Vice Prime Minister and Minister of Defense Jaber al-Mubarak al-Hamad Al-Sabah, a member of the ruling family, who is currently Prime Minister. He began by saying that his main concern was the instability in neighboring Iraq, to which he could see no end, and which, in fact, was getting worse and worse. Compared to the Americans, the British forces responsible for the Basra border area were using more conciliatory strategies towards the local population, but this was not enough. The confusion was such that the various competing local groups could not even be easily linked to specific political views.

The country was experiencing a conflagration that raged everywhere and anywhere. At that time, it seemed so hopeless that little Kuwait feared being infected by it. Not surprisingly, he mentioned that priority should be given to urgently needed training for the Iraqi armed forces. He displayed unqualified interest in the initiative I was promoting. It was not surprising that he saw combating terrorism and the reform of the national defense system as a priority.

From the very beginning, I had to make clear that the Alliance neither sold nor supplied military equipment. This was the responsibility of individual countries, and Kuwait had to make its own independent choices. Instead, what the Alliance was doing, and where it had recognized value, was the reform of armed forces in accordance with modern organizational principles. This was an activity at which it excelled, and was intended in the first instance to improve the efficiency of its own members. These were activities and procedures proven by years of experience. The Minister of Defense promised to send a mission to Brussels in the near future to learn about it.

Minister of Foreign Affairs Abbas Abu Hassan received me in traditional dress, and said that our message was welcome because the initiative promoted greater regional stability. He had read the document approved by the heads of state and government in Istanbul, and in his view it contained all that was required to do whatever was needed together. In brief, it was very much in Kuwait's interest to welcome NATO's political initiative in this fragile strategic area.

He was curious about NATO's mission in a remote place like

Afghanistan. This gave me the opportunity to reply that Atlantic Alliance operations had always, in fact, been aimed at helping Muslim populations in trouble, from Bosnia to Kosovo, from Macedonia to Afghanistan. This demolished the stereotype of Western military organizations with hostile intentions toward the Islamic world. When this issue was raised, initial skepticism was usually followed by an embarrassed silence.

Part of the strategy I had envisaged for my contacts in the region was not to limit myself to government representatives. A round table was organized in a modern and pleasant setting with professors and students from the American University of Kuwait. At one point, the Minister of Petroleum also made an appearance. A major daily Arabic language newspaper, *Al-Rai al Alaam*, covered the events.

To confirm this political line in January 2017 Kuwait opened a Nato training center devoted to regional cooperation.

Although we found great cordiality and a friendly reception, we still had to deal with unexpected ways of doing things. In the Gulf, I had to become accustomed to schedules that involved a high degree of improvisation.

Sometimes the local flexibility honestly proved to be too much. Later on, I happened to go to Qatar for negotiations, and was surprised by the absence of interlocutors. It was immediately apparent that there had been some confusion, and the authorities thought I was there to attend military exercises that were taking place at that time. Nothing could have been further from my mind. Fortunately, Qatar's Mohammed Al-Rumaihi, then a senior Foreign Ministry official responsible for follow-up with NATO, currently Minister of Municipality and Environment, is an efficient man, and within a matter of minutes the visit was brought back on track.

In the early days, I reacted badly. Then I got so used to this style that I now recommend patience and flexibility to all those who deal with that part of the world. With experience, you learn that things can work differently from place to place, and that it is not so difficult to adapt.

After the interesting and meaningful visit to Kuwait, my next stop was the United Arab Emirates, another destination I was visiting for the first time. It is larger country than Kuwait, with fewer problems with difficult and aggressive neighbors, but also with an implicit threat. Iran is directly across the Gulf, and I could glimpse its snow-capped mountains from the plane as I flew over the Gulf. It came to mind that even some Roman emperors had died fighting against the ancient Persians. Today, ignoring protests, Tehran militarily occupies some islands that traditionally belonged to Abu Dhabi.

What clearly stands out is the imbalance of power between Iran and the UAE; the latter would be an easy prey. This explains why the Gulf states are hesitant to openly criticize their powerful neighbor, whether it concerns the atomic bomb, territorial claims, or other issues. In private, the attitude is very different, and concerns about the expansionist ambitions of the ayatollahs are expressed in no uncertain terms with foreign interlocutors.

The Persian Gulf, or Arabian Gulf if you prefer, is relatively narrow, especially at the geopolitically sensitive Strait of Hormuz, and seems almost a large lake. From the rugged Iranian desert coastline, it is possible to see the gas flares of oil wells on the other shore, as well as the lights of the large international hotels and luxury supermarkets. Inevitably these represent a natural target, temptation for a large and populous country in economic difficulty.

In Abu Dhabi, I was greeted by military protocol officials, and had no idea to whom I would be talking. A senior officer took me to a government residence, a secluded villa, announcing that the next day I would be given full details. I had become used to state residences, starting in Bulgaria, where I was hosted together with Italian Defense Minister Andreatta, in a sinister isolated mansion near Sofia. I was given an entire apartment for one night. I still remember the terrible cold I suffered, and how I had never been so happy to see the morning. I told the Minister about my feelings about this, and he admitted that had felt exactly the same.

Such residences are intentionally ideal buildings for security, because they are fenced and have armed guards. Common features are that they are half-empty and generally decorated with replicas of antique furniture. In Abu Dhabi that evening, I was given a huge suite where, as always, a procession of multicolored soft drinks lined the bar.

The next day I met with representatives from the Ministry of

Foreign Affairs and the Ministry of Defense but not the two ministers, who apparently were out of the country. It is a fact of diplomatic life that members of governments are often abroad for official or personal reasons. In fact, it would seem that such missions are quite popular with those involved. Before leaving Europe, we had to decide whether we would carry out the missions without the guarantee of seeing the relevant ministers themselves. In general, I decided to take the risk. For logistical and organizational reasons, my visits usually covered several countries, and this was a way to spread out chances for high-level meetings.

I had met UAE Deputy Minister of Foreign Affairs Abdullah Al-Nahyan in Brussels, which he remembered. He had a positive opinion of the official proposal approved in Istanbul, and appreciated the fact that I had come so far to confirm what had been said during our first meeting at the Hotel Conrad.

However, it was necessary, in his view, to go further, and he proposed an initiative aimed at the press and local media to make NATO better known. This is something that I repeated in every country in the region, since it was clear we were unknown and had never been regarded as a potential partner. It must be said that NATO was not the best in adapting to these circumstances, and it took considerable effort to improve our public diplomacy.

Al-Nahyan was very explicit about the strategic importance of his country and the dangers it faced. They were afraid of Tehran. The increase in Iran's military capabilities and its nuclear program went hand in hand with its militant ideology and the historic ambition for expansion towards neighboring countries, which dated back to the time of the Shah.

In second place was concern about Iraq, where the borders were by now uncontrolled and gave greater freedom of movement to terrorist groups of various persuasions. In fact, anyone who wanted to enter Iraq could do so without any problem. His conclusion was that rebuilding the Iraqi security forces was a priority, not only for Iraq, but also for its neighbors. For the first time, I also heard concerns about the internal situation in Saudi Arabia, the root causes being the lack of internal reforms and the potential instability of their system of government. This was of concern to the other Gulf countries, which feared a domino effect.

I used the usual mantra, i.e. that the UAE could continue bilateral cooperation agreements with whomever they wanted. By representing so many influential governments all together, the Alliance simply sought to provide added value. We also should remember that the United States, a NATO member, is in fact guarantor of the territorial integrity of all these countries, and has sizeable military bases in the area. Their strategic importance has grown with the operations in Afghanistan. Basically, all supplies for Kabul pass through here. There are no alternatives.

In accepting the Afghan challenge, we found ourselves in hot water from a logistical viewpoint as well. Kabul is one of the most expensive destinations in the world for transporting personnel and equipment. For example, the Italian Air Force had its hub in Abu Dhabi. There you changed planes and after 4-5 hours in a C-130 you could be in Kabul, after flying over a serious quantity of desert.

Returning to talks in the UAE capital, Chief of Staff of the Armed Forces Hamad Al-Rumaithy seemed well aware of the scenarios I had described. For this reason, his priorities were very specific. You often find that the military are more frank than politicians. He was very friendly, and brought up the positive experience his country's forces had had in the Balkans, e.g. in the NATO peacekeeping mission in Kosovo, known as KFOR.

He was direct in saying that the security of his region could not be left only to the locals, the response had to be from everyone, and the Western community had historic responsibilities from which it could not escape. The general made it clear that, in discussions with the Arabs, the West moved too quickly, giving them the impression of wanting to use them for our own purposes, and not to win their hearts and minds. He was right.

The Chief of Staff did not hesitate in stating that the greatest threat to peace and stability was the unresolved Arab-Israeli conflict. He had a point. He added that Iran and its aggressive nuclear program, as well as the situation in Iraq, were potentially destructive for the rest of the region.

It was interesting that, although criticism rained down on the United States, no one had given up on the shield of American protection. Europe was sometimes talked about, but as a "soft power," very important in commercial, cultural, and social fields, but not for international security.

Al-Rumaithy informed me that the chiefs of staff in the region had decided to send a joint delegation to Brussels, in order to explore the actual potential of things that could be done together. Their ultimate goal could be to participate together in operations, but to reach that point it would be necessary to consolidate their training and procedures. The addition of new security providers was a prerequisite for expanded world governance.

I continued my trip in Dubai, with a conference at the Gulf Research Center, a privately funded think tank, and an interview with the *Al-Khaleej* newspaper. In visiting the Center, I saw that they could afford top-level resources, and there were German, Dutch, and English researchers working at the center. They explained that they were in close contact with the principal international political think tanks. These networks are not to be underestimated, since they can be good incubators for ideas. Dubai, however, seemed to me an artificial place, with not much soul, where everything was counted in hard cash, even the air. A center of modern day tourism and finance, as fashionable as it is fragile. Any international crisis could easily bring it down.

I found Bahrain more exciting. It is a small country with few resources, next to greedy and powerful neighbors. They need to have sharp wits and keep their eyes peeled to survive. The art of survival becomes important in a rough neighborhood, where it would take only one false step for this group of islands to be swallowed in one bite. The Al-Khalifa royal family is obliged to do something with international networks to get noticed, which they actively do.

Like other the Gulf countries, the State of Bahrain, just off the coast of the Arabian Peninsula, was at one time a British protectorate. Historically, its only profitable activity was pearl fishing in the adjacent sea. The locus of the Shiite uprising in 2011 was, in fact, the Pearl Roundabout, and the rising as a result was christened the Pearl Revolution.

Our reception in Manama was purposefully cordial, with a certain, somewhat ostentatious, Western level of comfort. While waiting to complete the registration formalities in my hotel after my long trip, I asked for something to drink, meaning water.

Unexpectedly, I was immediately presented with a hefty glass of whiskey, as though a secret code had been triggered. I then learned that the big hotels in Bahrain are frequented by Saudis, who can get there directly by highway, crossing a bridge that gives them easy access to the islands. The influx of tourists increases during the weekends, encouraged by the fact that, unlike in the Saudi kingdom, you can freely sin, at least as regards the purchase of alcohol.

With its base in the port of Manama, the US Fifth Fleet is considered the best guarantee for the country's survival. There is even a Formula One race track. Everything and anything to gain visibility, and to be useful. If one day a powerful neighbor seeks to swallow up Bahrain, the international community will take notice.

I met with King Hamad bin Isa Al-Khalifa, who explained his vision of the region. He is keen-eyed, friendly, and direct. We met in a small elegant pavilion overlooking a garden full of greenery. I still have a pleasant memory of this meeting.

It seemed natural for me to say to him that, for a country of limited resources such as Bahrain, it was a good idea to be involved with a prominent international organization that could offer much more than individual powers taken singularly. Within the Atlantic Alliance, as a whole, it was possible to find a diverse range of experience and abilities, from which Bahrain could choose the ones best suited to its needs.

Trying to seize the moment, I said that such a relationship offered the best guarantee for Bahrain's security. I explained that NATO's political decisions were taken by a consensus of allied governments and that, for this reason, it was very difficult to take up any hostile initiative towards anyone, especially a partner. I concluded by saying the Alliance took its decisions independently, but that, in fact, all operations decided in the last decade had had the support of the UN Security Council. In other words, they had legitimacy.

These arguments seemed to persuade the King, who replied that he welcomed the initiative, given its potential in terms of new security areas for Bahrain.

He realized that this would not compromise existing relationships with Washington or London, and therefore represented added value. The King commented that, on one hand, there was the United States, with all its military and economic wealth, its desire to do things, but with insufficient experience in his part of the world. On the other hand, there were the European states, rich in traditions, with a good knowledge of the Middle East, but unwilling to take action that would involve political responsibility and high costs.

Given the geographic location of the islands, the priority was the security of shipping lanes, bearing in mind that the oil traffic in the Gulf is of vital importance for the whole world. The sovereign said he would very much favor hosting a NATO naval base. It seemed that he could see a future guarantee for the kingdom's political integrity that was way beyond any intentions we then had or commitments that we could then make.

The next step was the modernization of the Bahrain Defense Force, providing it more advanced technologies. After all, there were other small states, like Singapore, that possessed significant self-defense capabilities.

Both the King and the Crown Prince did not conceal their concern about being at the center of an area of political instability. Not the least was the situation in Saudi Arabia. There, the introduction of reforms was coming late, and the political system had serious difficulties in addressing the questions that inevitably arose with the modernization of the country.

The King was clearly of the view that civil society should not be subordinated to religion. Otherwise the whole system of government would be put into jeopardy. His criticism was implicit, expressed without raising controversy. According to him, extremism had different causes, depending on the political context in which it arose. In Pakistan it was because of poverty, and in Palestine it was due to the Israeli occupation.

From this reasoning, it followed that cooperation with NATO would contribute to stability in the region, especially on practical issues that he felt were not receiving sufficient attention. The King and the Crown Prince said explicitly that this was one more reason why Bahrain should become an international center where great political issues were discussed.

They had in mind organizing conferences on security with the participation of leading world figures. A contribution by the Alliance to this initiative would be most welcome. I later found out that large sums were being paid to the International Institute for Strategic Studies in London to organize some interesting events.

Crown Prince Salman Hamad Al-Khalifa, who had the reputation to be a reformer, dwelled on an aspect that we certainly
could agree on. Namely, that it was necessary to provide a practical framework for these ideas, otherwise they would slowly disappear into thin air, as had happened to many other initiatives, even
those begun with the best intentions. He promised that, in the near
future, he would send a delegation to Brussels to look into these
opportunities. I left after two interviews in Manama, one with *Al-
Ayam* and the other with the *Bahrain Tribune*, which showed how
much the leadership wanted to prepare public opinion for these
new contacts.

Unlike in the other Gulf states, the majority of the population
in Bahrain is Shiite, while the royal family is Sunni. At the time of
my first trip, the King had decided to give the Shiites some official
recognition. This was the result of pressure from the Crown Prince,
who was considered a reformist. He was about 35 years old, a graduate of American University in Washington, DC, and had obtained
a doctorate in history at Cambridge.

He wanted to let us know that a member of the Shiite community had been named a cabinet minister. Jawad Salem Al-Arrayed
became Minister of Justice in 2002, and since 2006 has been Deputy
Prime Minister. Today, however, we understand that this has not
been enough to placate the Shiite community.

At that time, the degree of discontent was unclear. It was a
problem that was smoldering and ready to ignite, but little was said
about it. When in February 2011 the Shiite uprising broke out, it
caused great surprise, as the country was not on the map of "trouble spots." Demonstrations continued for several days in the main
squares of Manama before being harshly suppressed. Saudi Arabia
came to the rescue by sending a military contingent, while other
Gulf countries contributed with police units.

The situation was very delicate for the United States. On the one
hand, the Obama administration clearly was signaling to Bahrain
the need to reform. This was also the case in Egypt, Libya, and elsewhere. On the other hand, it was not easy to criticize a country like
Bahrain that was friendly enough to host the American fleet.

In conclusion, it is clear from what I have described that the
Gulf countries are important and fragile at the same time. Despite

a rich local history, the peoples of the area became of interest to the West only rather recently and for clearly circumscribed reasons, i.e. the presence of petroleum resources. In order to secure and preserve their independence, they have had to evolve more rapidly than their European counterparts in the past, with dramatic impacts on deeply rooted local tradition. A difficult challenge.

As fate would have it, in addition to possessing oil and economic affluence, these countries are located in a thorny geographical position that exposes them to many risks.

It is therefore almost a necessity to find protectors, a role played for many years by the United States of America. This forced those involved to periodically perform political pirouettes to reconcile this obvious and understandable reality with their full-blown support for the cause of the Palestinian people.

These monarchies would like a formal guarantee of their integrity from the West. It is what they would like from the Atlantic Alliance as well as from the United States. But this requires skillful compromises, since no one in Brussels is realistically prepared to go to war to defend Bahrain or Qatar. These are quiet echoes of the questions that European democracies were asking themselves when faced with the threat to Poland by Hitler in 1939: Was it worth dying for Danzig? What about Manama? The other side of the equation, however, is that this region does have two-thirds of the world's oil reserves, not to mention that Qatar that is among the world's leading producers of natural gas, which it exports by sea around the globe.

Egypt: Always a Special Case

Given the fluidity of Middle Eastern politics, it was necessary to demonstrate pragmatism. Having built with difficulty the ground floor of our partnership architecture, the next objective was to involve Egypt. As already noted, Egypt is a key country in the Arab world, the link between the Mediterranean, Africa, and the Arabian Peninsula. Those in power in Cairo find themselves at the crossroads of several worlds, a textbook geopolitical challenge.

In 2004 no one would have imagined the events of Tahrir Square, the change to the constitution, the tumultuous events that led the country to a new and unexpected balance of power that ended, after 16 months of tension, with the election of Mohammed Morsi, a member of the Muslim Brotherhood, as president, followed later by a military takeover. Whatever takes place on the banks of the Nile is always of relevance for other countries in the region. The break in the tradition of having military officers as president probably was too brief, however, to end up having much influence elsewhere.

At the time of my mission, two very important figures were General Omar Soliman, chief of the intelligence services, and Marshal Mohammed Tantawi, Minister of Defense, who later became the interim head of state following Mubarak's fall from power. As we have seen, they did not want to break off Egypt's very limited relationship with NATO, but neither did they want to give the impression of becoming involved in matters that seemed to have too Western a stamp. In the conspiracy theories that reigned supreme, it was assumed that someone who said one thing actually was thinking of something quite different. Perhaps they imagined that we wanted to become involved in the Israeli-Palestinian issue, by proposing ourselves as a peacekeeping force.

NATO Secretary General de Hoop Scheffer was worried about this, and I had a difficult time convincing him that Egypt's position was not definitive. Arab ambassador friends whispered in my ear that Egypt would avoid being isolated, and that my efforts should not be conditioned by the Egyptians. I took their advice to heart and continued an open dialogue with Cairo, while passing on the message that we were going ahead with or without them.

This was another occasion when I was able to verify that, behind a facade of solidarity, within the Arab world there are different interests and distinct rivalries. Algeria, for example, resents Egypt's political primacy in the Mediterranean. The Algerians see themselves as natural leaders because of their trans-Saharan dimension and their energy resources. Algeria also believes it demonstrated its resilience in its war of liberation from France.

To renew contacts with the Egyptians, we thought about a joint public diplomacy initiative with the main forum for discussion of foreign policy in Cairo, the Egyptian Council for Foreign Affairs. A gathering place for the ruling class, its headquarters is an elegant building near the Nile, where official receptions are held for distinguished guests under the patronage of the Ministry of Foreign Affairs. It was agreed that we would discuss the issue of regional stability and how to open new avenues for progress. The conference took place in early 2005, with significant public participation and an interesting debate following the Foreign Minister's introduction and my speech. This time I had the blessing of the Ambassador to Brussels, Mahmoud Karem, an influential and able diplomat.

I began to learn that Middle Eastern public opinion is frustrated, because it feels subjected to the policies of others who have different interests, without being able to turn the tables. The questions asked of Western speakers always concern the West's lack of support for the Palestinian cause and its allegedly unconditional assistance for Israel, while pretending not to see Israel's nuclear capability, its indifference to Arab peace plans, and its preconceived hostility towards Iran.

Cairo is special for many things, historical, environmental, etc. It is a megalopolis with indescribable traffic, Stalinist style buildings alongside old crumbling palaces. In short, an extraordinary urbanistic confusion. Nevertheless, it is pleasant, not hostile, and you get used to its challenges. Cairo's greatest visual asset is the Nile, a fascinating river flowing along completely unaware of what is taking place on its banks, giving an overall air of grandeur to the city.

This time I was formally received, in a very courteous manner, by the Minister of Foreign Affairs, youthful, handsome, and elegant in appearance. During our meeting, we were able to go over all aspects of the relations between NATO and the land of the pyramids. The headquarters of Egyptian diplomacy is equal to its ambitions, an attractive, airy modern building overlooking the great river.

Ahmed Aboul Gheit had been ambassador in Rome, and emphasized how much he had liked his time in Italy. Rome is home to the most beautiful Egyptian embassy, Villa Savoia, which used to be the residence of the Italian royal family. The last Italian king gave it to the Egyptians, with all its furnishings, as a sign of gratitude for having been warmly welcomed in Alexandria after the fall of the monarchy.

I had waited for this opportunity to dispel misconceptions and to finally clarify with the government not only the potential, but also the limitations in developing a new friendship. I knew that this meeting was a rare opportunity to leave a mark, so I tried to cover the most difficult topics. The distrust of Egyptian public opinion towards Western initiatives, which were seen as a kind of bear hug, was well known.

It seemed to me that I hit the right note when I mentioned that Egypt had nothing to fear from an international organization where the rule was consensus and everything had to be agreed upon. Moreover, our new watchword was "let's be practical" without creating new obligations.

Yes, it is true that there would be a framework of multilateral meetings in which everyone would participate, including Israel. But Cairo recognized the Jerusalem government, so the only embarrassment might be a little extra publicity. On the other hand, including everyone in meetings was an obligatory precondition to put everyone on an equal footing by making the same offers to all.

I tried to make it clear to Aboul Gheit that it would be in his interest to expand the game by creating more tables where diverse interlocutors could sit. I said right away that the Alliance had absolutely no intention of touching the raw nerve of Arab-Israeli relations. There was no political consensus on the subject even among NATO member countries. Therefore, I did not represent a fifth column of hidden interests.

The mantra that I was authorized to repeat was that a direct NATO military role in the territories of Israel and a Palestinian State would only be possible under three conditions: a peace agreement; the explicit request of all parties; a Security Council resolution. This was a framework that would not cause any unwanted political side effects for our interlocutors.

The Minister was skillful and polished, saying that up till then he had maintained a reserved attitude because he had wanted to see the entire framework more clearly. Now that he understood the goals of the Western initiative better, he felt comfortable in supporting it.

He then gave me a lecture that I heard repeated many times on the banks of the Nile: "We come, but do not accelerate too much, do things gradually. We follow, but not necessarily always at the same pace, this will depend on the politics of the time." With the corollary: "But do not worry."

He then provided the other caveat that I heard repeated everywhere, albeit with different accents. Namely, it was important to be more proactive and explain things well to the Arabic language media, following the same lines of reasoning that we had shared in our meeting. In this he was completely right. The "Egyptian Street" was pretty hostile, in contrast to the elites who had a broader view. Whether we liked it or not, Westerners were not loved, because they were perceived as innately imperialistic, still smelling of colonialism. In order not to throw more fuel onto the fire, it was necessary to talk, explain things to society, and to try to win it over.

He fervently advised me to emphasize the principle that I had illustrated to him, namely cooperation as "a two-way street" rather than the "one-way street" of the past, now firmly rejected. I agreed with him and tried to follow his advice in a series of local television and newspaper interviews.

From my point of view, the outcome of the visit was definitely positive. What could this success be attributed to? A real conviction, perhaps helped by the way things had been presented? Was it the weight of the Western world behind the Alliance that had impressed Cairo? Or was it that they simply thought it was better not to obstruct a process that would go ahead regardless? These questions were all the more justified given that even Western governments involved had doubts about the success of their own proposals. Aboul Gheit's own talents as a diplomat certainly were another important factor. I was pleased, though not surprised, when the Arab League appointed him Secretary General in 2016, and I had the pleasure of meeting with him again in his new capacity.

On the way back to Europe I attempted to put in order the thousands of impressions I had collected that confirmed how difficult it was to decipher a different world. I was in a privileged position to better understand the interests, fears, and considerations of the various parties. Not everyone could have such a broad picture of the situation.

It was difficult, however, to organize and then convey this highly complex data, since everything in an international organization ends up in procedures that tend to smooth things over, giving the impression that one problem is the same as another.

The permanent representatives to the North Atlantic Council approved my report on the mission with some surprise at the outcomes, as had been the case with my earlier consultations. I frankly had expected more discussion of Egypt and its apparent policy shift regarding NATO's outreach, given the importance of the country. It is true, however, that capitals already had had the chance to mull over the briefing I had provided to the NATO country embassies in Cairo.

At this point, given that an overall picture was beginning to take shape, involving a dozen or so governments, it became necessary to think seriously about the practical instruments to achieve the stated objectives. They had to be as simple as possible, to avoid wasting endless time in discussing procedures, as was often the case. Instead, the priority was to attain real and visible results, which required clear instructions to the International Staff.

In complex organizations like NATO, it is only possible to do things effectively by applying strong pressure from above. Policy lines must be constantly reconfirmed, otherwise new events or emergencies inevitably intervene and direct attention elsewhere. Since the end of the Cold War, the Atlantic Alliance had been focused on enlargement towards Eastern Europe and attentive to relations with the countries of the former Soviet Union, devoting great energy to those challenges. For my part, I tried instead to represent continuity in our efforts with North Africa and the Middle East. In this, I was fortunate to have the full support of the Secretary General and influential permanent representatives.

Saudi Arabia, the Core of the Gulf Region

While travelling by car in a distant country, I received a call from the Saudi ambassador in Brussels, Nasser Al-Assaf. "His Royal Highness the Crown Prince would like to see you this afternoon", he announced.

"Where? " I asked instinctively. "In Riyadh, of course", he replied, with the air of someone who was stating the obvious. I explained that I was honored by the invitation from the heir to the throne Prince Abdullah (later King from 2005 to 2015), but that it was impossible for me to get to the capital in time, i.e. just a few hours later. The matter ended there, but it is indicative of a certain worldview found in Riyadh, and a good introduction to my story.

The kingdom of the Al Saud dynasty - Custodians of the Two Holy Mosques - occupies a special place in the Middle East for its size, its strategic location, and its resources. On one hand, it has huge oil reserves, which the advanced countries cannot do without. On the other hand, its financial resources are such that it is one of the most courted customers.

Riyadh looks out on the world without any desire to conform to the standards of others. In 1924 the House of Saud, a tribe of warriors, completed the re-conquest of the country by occupying Mecca, where the Hashemite dynasty had reigned since 1201, albeit for several centuries as hereditary governors under the Ottoman Empire's control. The last representative of the Hashemites sits on the throne in Amman.

Members of the Saudi royal family, and other prominent Saudis, study at the best universities and can obtain assistance from the most cutting-edge consultants available on the market. They can rely on the best advice and technology. However, it is also the only country in the Arab world to have a religious police that punishes all infractions.

Women live in a world apart, indeed the male visitor finds himself face to face with a male universe. On my first trip to Riyadh, I remember my naïve surprise at seeing signs indicating separate prayer rooms for men and women inside the magnificent modern airport.

The AlSaud family rules with a firm hand, buttressed, in their own view, by long tradition. It is a large family with numerous princes and cousins, each of whom has a comparative advantage in one thing or another. On one hand, they provide support for the monarchy, but, on the other hand, can be a burden.

Of course, the members of the royal family are not the only high-status members of Saudi society. Other elements of the Saudi elite include merchants, administrators, and intellectual authorities, both religious and secular. Then there are the immigrants, often highly qualified technicians who remain outside the decision-making processes.

Riyadh is a major player in the surrounding region and in the world. It has an active foreign policy and is considered a counterweight to Iran. It boasts a well-trained diplomatic service with abundant resources at its disposal. By today's standards, however, the Kingdom is moving ahead at a slow pace, too slow to avoid criticism.

A few years earlier, in fact, during the visit to Italy of Saudi Minister of Defense Prince Sultan, later Crown Prince, Italian Defense Minister Andreatta and I had found ourselves reflecting on the shortage of substantive content in our talks. At Milan's Malpensa Airport, Prince Sultan disembarked from a Boeing loaded with assistants and attended a helicopter demonstration by the Agusta company, but displayed a visible lack of interest.

The United States is essentially the guarantor of Saudi Arabia's security. It has bases in the country and is the main supplier of military technology. As a result, there is a privileged bilateral political relationship and the Saudi ambassador in Washington is a high-profile figure.

The first summit meeting with the United States, between

Franklin Roosevelt and King Abdul Aziz ibn Saud, happened in a very unusual way. The meeting was held in 1945, near the end of World War II, in secret aboard the USS *Quincy* on a lake in the Suez Canal. The King went in secret to the port of Jeddah with a retinue of two hundred people who wanted to board the destroyer USS *Murphy*, which was to take them to the *Quincy*. The American commander had to deal with space limitations, however, and finally decided to allow only 43 people aboard, after agitated negotiations.

The political understanding between the two leaders was immediate. Both had something to gain and the foundations of a strategic alliance were laid. The complementarity of this relationship favored its success and continues to this day.

The Saudi Kingdom also tries to maintain good relations with other Islamic countries, and even with unfriendly movements, to safeguard themselves from all angles. For example, the Saudis financed the largest mosque in Pakistan. They actively support religious instruction in European mosques. This is often criticized by Muslims who believe the Saudis are promoting forms of Islam specific to the Arabian Peninsula that are very different from North African traditions of Islam. Substantial sums of money are handed out as charity to groups of various different kinds. It is difficult sometimes to track down the real origins and goals of these groups.

For us it was clear that Saudi Arabia was the most important of the potential partners in the Gulf region. Of great importance, but also complex and vulnerable. After meeting Minister of Foreign Affairs Prince Saud Al-Faisal in Brussels, the question was whether or not to go to Riyadh. I knew it would be difficult, though, and therefore set it aside until we could do an ad hoc trip.

Despite all our preparations, it turned out to be very complicated, precisely because it was the first approach. The Saudi ambassador in Brussels was very kind on a formal level, and even slightly intimidated by the attention he was getting from NATO. Having been in charge of civil aviation in Saudi Arabia, he was an important figure in the country. However, he could not get responses from his capital.

Over time, I came to understand that the Ministry of Foreign Affairs and the Ministry of Defense were two different worlds, and had difficult relations with each other. In addition, you had to be on the same wavelength as the Royal House. This was a complex context in which to work. Few people were in a position to forge the required consensus.

A formal invitation to visit finally arrived. A sort of preparatory dinner was given in my honor at the elegant residence of the Saudi chief of mission in Brussels, with the whole group of Arab ambassadors in attendance. The dinner was strictly for men, with no alcoholic beverages served. I noticed that the host had the air of being "the first among equals" with his colleagues, albeit with great cordiality, even some fairly boisterous jocularity. The other guests expressed a respectful formal brotherhood. It was clear that Saudi Arabia was the hub of the region.

However, I was not able to get any idea about what meetings were being planned in Riyadh, and the problem was clearly evident when I landed in Riyadh the next day. The delegation and I were taken to a prestigious looking but semi-deserted government residence used for official guests. After we had spent the night there, the next morning the protocol officials said they were organizing some meetings, but did not mention any names.

After a few hours, I started to get annoyed and got on the phone with Ambassador Nasser Al-Assaf in Brussels, the only lifeline available. He was clearly embarrassed and assured me that he would do everything possible. He indicated that the top figures in the government system were abroad that day. This is how I learned that there were three protocol services — Ministry of Foreign Affairs, Ministry of Defense, and the Royal House — that had to coordinate with each other. This certainly did not make things easy. After having waited a long time, I decided that it was just too much, and informed our motorcade escort that I would be leaving the country, with the responsibility for an inconclusive visit laid at the door of the local authorities.

At that point, I was told that a very senior official at the Ministry of Foreign Affairs, Prince Turki bin Mohammed bin Saud Al Kabeer, was waiting for me. I was irritated, and made no attempt to hide from him my surprise at the treatment I had received. He in turn was totally unaware that I had had to wait for half a day. He asked his assistants for confirmation of this, and they duly nodded. In the end, he formally apologized on behalf of the royal family. I never managed to find out whether there had been political problems that day or simply a case of bureaucratic misunderstandings.

In any case, I finally was able to have a substantive conversation. Prince Turki described in detail the initiatives launched by Saudi Arabia for peace and against nuclear proliferation in the Middle East. He clearly stated that the Ministry of Foreign Affairs was interested in exploring the opportunities for cooperation that NATO could offer.

To show our seriousness, I left him a number of documents that I had brought along, including a list of activities planned for partners. I invited him to come to Brussels to acquire first-hand any other information that might be considered useful.

In fact, the Prince paid a visit to Brussels a few weeks later. I took care in preparing a formal reception for him, including reserving a room for the delegation to pray at the prescribed times. He seemed satisfied with the outcome of his meetings, saying he would give us a written reply.

PART TWO

So far, I have focused on the process of laying the political foundations for NATO cooperation with the great, but complex, Arab world. I turn now to the process of building a common architecture. An architecture worthy of the name, but light enough to take into consideration the region's diversity, and visions that often diverge from those of the West.

This break with the first part of this book is due to the fact that this was no longer the initial stage, i.e. that of the first approach. At this point in the narrative, initiatives had been launched, and we were in an ongoing search for added value to give to our partners, not only to be of use to them, but to draw them closer to us in a common vision of global stability. This is good for us and everyone else, since balance and an overall framework will help create greater world harmony.

At the end, there is an epilogue on how international society functions. Too little is known about this, and it may be useful to the reader in understanding the most important issues facing today's world. It analyzes the dynamic of events from the standpoint of international organizations, which operate quite differently from national governments.

Israel at the Center of the Region

Having made the rounds of the forest, trying to measure all the trees, it was clear that one tree was in a sense larger than them all, and of extreme importance for all the others. Jerusalem was obviously a unique player, given the high level of its infrastructure, efficient bureaucracy, and its ability to make choices based on a 360-degree perspective.

Israel had no strong views on to how to build an effective relationship with NATO. Historically, there had been little contact between us. The Alliance had been engaged in the Cold War, while Israel's existence was at stake in a largely different context.

Still, while the Arabs sensed a pro-American wind blowing in from Brussels and instinctively took precautions, in Jerusalem there were no negative preconceptions. Clearly, however, the Israeli vision of this initiative was speculative, and there was no particular sympathy for it.

The Israeli ambassador in Brussels, Oded Eran, was a person of substance. He was born in Israel and his wife came from a great Polish rabbinical family. He now is engaged in academic pursuits. I established a close personal relationship with him, and therefore was able to enlarge the scope of our discussions. He was completely in favor of setting up a real partnership, as he saw the advantages of having another link to the West, while expanding Israel's relations with Arab countries in a multilateral context. I believe he was right.

He understood that a high-profile international organization held within it an added value that could be beneficial. He was also an excellent negotiator. One day he told me how he had managed to get Israel included in European research programs. Apparently, he had taken the French prime minister off guard during a visit to Jerusalem, and the prime minister was then unable to retract the promise he had made in a moment of distraction.

I was able to convince him that his country should play along and not seek disproportionate advantages, since the offer of cooperation was addressed to everyone without distinction. In that case, the Arabs would have thought they were being put on the back burner, but, in reality they were just slower in moving, less certain of their priorities, and burdened with less efficient bureaucracies.

An Atlantic Forum was formed in Israel, certainly a move not to be underestimated. The person behind this initiative was Uzi Arad, a former senior officer of Mossad. Later, he became the director of Israel's National Security Council in the Benjamin Netanyahu government. The newly formed Israeli Atlantic Forum decided to sponsor an international conference, with ambitious goals for visibility also within the country. Jerusalem is influential in the network of international think tanks, and therefore able to count on people at the highest levels, and substantial financial resources. Herzliya, a well-known seaside resort north of Tel Aviv, was chosen as the site of this event.

I could hardly turn down an invitation to be the keynote speaker at the conference. However, knowing a little about Israel, I was worried that I might find myself in a difficult situation, in which the press would not hesitate in giving the outside world the message they preferred. I had noticed that the Israeli press often interpreted events and the statements of foreign guests from a domestic viewpoint.

There was certainly no lack of issues to address: the Iranian nuclear bomb, the Palestinian crisis following the Intifada, terrorism, Hamas, Hezbollah and so on. It was therefore impossible to keep a low profile. They would expect a high-ranking representative from Brussels to express his opinions on big, hot issues. They planned a televised debate and a press conference with Minister of Foreign Affairs Tzipi Livni, in addition to bilateral discussions.

NATO only had limited expertise with the aforementioned issues, beyond staunch opposition to the proliferation of weapons of mass destruction, and within the Alliance there were generally no shared positions on these issues. This made it impossible for me to take any formal positions. It often is forgotten that a political-military alliance can only act on what has been agreed among its members, that is, the member governments.

The Public Affairs Division of the NATO International Staff insisted I should only speak on issues in which NATO had direct competence. I decided otherwise, since I would not be taken seriously if I simply ignored problems that were on everyone's lips (like Iran), even if it meant taking some risks. For a few days, I studied the main issues, the national positions and their content, even though I knew that I could not make political judgments where I was not authorized.

Then-Foreign Minister Livni had an authoritative manner and projected competence. She too had served in Mossad. It seemed, in fact, that having been in Mossad was almost a sign of intellectual distinction. She seemed completely natural, telling me that, as a mother, she was worried about her twenty-year-old son, who was doing his military service in the Navy. Ambassador Eran was present at the formal meeting, where we discussed Nato-Israel relations.

As expected, the debate with the public and the press was centered on Iran and weapons of mass destruction. I argued that it was to Israel's benefit to follow the general thinking of the international community against the proliferation of nuclear armaments, rather than seeking individual national military solutions, which would inevitably isolate it from the rest of the world. I noted that Javier Solana, then the European Union's representative for foreign policy, held regular meetings with Iranian negotiators together with France, Germany, and the United Kingdom. In the judgment of my colleagues, I passed the test quite satisfactorily. In the end, as we know, a nuclear agreement with Tehran was signed, though it took further years of hard work.

During those years, Israel did more than one zigzag in foreign policy, responding to changes in government coalitions and the fluctuating influence of the religious parties. My overall impression was that the country was used to living on the brink of a precipice, and to winning. It was therefore prepared to play a game of poker in which holding the losing cards might mean its own complete destruction.

It was arranged that I should meet the vice chairman of the Israel Atomic Energy Commission, a handsome man of about forty years of age. The fact that the country had the atom bomb was an open secret. In fact, there was a parliamentary committee for it that had a fictitious name. Sitting opposite me at a table in a wonderful restaurant overlooking the Herzliya marina, the Vice Chairman assured me that he moved in strict consultation with the intelligence services of France and the United Kingdom, and naturally also with those of the US. In his view Tehran would have the nuclear bomb in no time.

I was no newcomer to intelligence issues. For years, for example, I had received weekly briefings on the Balkans. These were generally so ominous that one day I asked the American official who was briefing me the reason for this approach, noting that events almost always contradicted the predictions. He chuckled in reply that he had to cover himself, and therefore it never did any harm to be a little more pessimistic than necessary.

My new friend from the Atomic Energy Commission, who had the air of someone from the same milieu, painted a gloomy picture of the leadership holding the reins in Tehran. He said that the mayor of the capital, later president, Mahmoud Ahmadinejad was a very devout Shiite, and, in accordance with the prophecies, was waiting from one moment to the next for the return of the Twelfth Imam or Mahdi. For this reason, he was busy having the Tehran's central avenues widened, so that, when he arrived, the Mahdi would find it easier to cross the capital with his knights. I wondered how much of this was true and how much was disinformation. Subsequently though, in 2012, President Ahmadinejad, in a speech to the UN General Assembly, did warn his audience to watch out, because the Twelfth Imam was on his way.

My Israeli interlocutor's main message was that NATO should be taking a leading role in dealing with this. I said that there were other players acting on behalf of the international community, and it was essential not to create confusion on such a sensitive matter. I also suggested that it was not the case to make too many assumptions about Tehran's exact intentions and plans for using a nuclear arsenal that was still in the works. The conversation ended there.

I had an unexpected problem with the Czech ambassador to

Israel, who maintained that Israel should become a member of NATO, a highly dangerous stance that could lead to serious mis-understandings. This extreme position surprised me, having spent several years in the dull atmosphere of Prague during the Cold War. I mentioned this to the Czech ambassador to NATO, Štefan Füle, who afterwards became a European Commissioner.

In the end, I left Tel Aviv with the sensation of having been pres-ent at a boxing match, with multiple rounds, in which the destiny of millions of people was at stake.

Oman, Between India and the Persian Gulf

The Sultan of Oman Qaboos Bin Said Al-Said keeps a low profile, although he is, at least in name, also Minister of Foreign Affairs, of Defense, and of Interior. He came to power in 1970, as a result of a bloodless coup against his father, not at all unusual in the region. The deposed Sultan then proceeded to live out the rest of his life in golden exile at the Hotel Savoy in London. The current sultan's lack of wives and children is something of a taboo subject, and he has entrusted the royal family with determining his eventual successor when the time comes.

Muscat, the far away capital of Oman, with its flower-lined avenues, gives one the sense of being in a different world, as compared to the other Gulf state capitals. The first difference is its geography, since the country is on the Indian Ocean, with only a small part that faces the Gulf of Oman, a sort of antechamber to the Strait of Hormuz. The local English-language newspapers write mainly about Pakistan and India. It is easy to understand why, since they are both directly across the Arabian Sea, the northwestern section of the Indian Ocean.

Another difference is that the history of Oman's relations with the West is older than that of all its neighboring countries, since it was on the main navigation routes between Europe, Africa, and Asia. Portuguese, Dutch, English and other navigators all passed through the country. It had an important role in the slave trade, as the Sultan also ruled Zanzibar, the center for the slave traffic in East Africa.

Oman has a long history as an independent state, going back to the 8th century A.D. The current ruling dynasty has been in power since the mid-1700s. But Oman is now less prosperous than its neighbors, as it has fewer energy resources.

Muscat is not a mass of ultramodern, if perhaps anonymous, buildings, like the capitals of other Gulf countries. The architecture is in a traditional style. Right behind the city, as one faces the sea, are tall mountains. Muscat looks like it would make a good movie set. The royal palace, with its colorful columns and wrought iron gates reminiscent of a French chateau, would not look entirely out of place in Hollywood.

This was the first time that NATO had ever set foot in that part of the world. Great effort had been made in preparing for the visit and much patience was needed. Relations with the sultanate's capital had to pass through the Omani ambassador in The Hague, Khadija Al-Lawati, and communications were not always easy.

Prior to arriving in Muscat, I had been travelling to other capitals in the region. Having received no replies from the Omanis, we contacted the British ambassador in Muscat to ask for his assistance.

I was in an unusual position, since I represented an international organization, not a government, and we did not have an office in the country. Therefore, we relied directly on the Omani government to organize political meetings and to book hotels, transport, and security.

After we finally received the assurances we had been waiting for, we landed in the capital. Our first meeting was with the British ambassador. The United Kingdom was clearly the country of reference for Oman. In fact, this was the only place where I happened on British officers in uniform. They provide assistance to the Omani army, which, for years, has had to deal with a guerrilla war on the border with Yemen in the perpetually troubled Hadramaut region. The Ambassador did not say much, not knowing how to interpret the novelty of a visit from NATO. However, he did tell us that it was quite clear that the authorities had only concerned themselves with our visit at the last moment.

I had a long meeting with Acting Minister of Foreign Affairs Yusuf bin Alawi bin Abdullah, an elegant and gracious man, with aristocratic features. His bright, flower-filled office was equally tasteful. Even today, senior members of the government carry beautifully crafted daggers, known as *khanjars*, on official occasions.

It was not an easy discussion, however, given that our interlocutors lacked basic knowledge on the international security system, and naturally also about NATO.

This required me to give a long disquisition on the historical development of the Alliance, the Cold War and the current attempt to form modern partnerships. It also wasn't easy to explain the added value of an international organization, with its Euro-Atlantic composition, for the security of Oman. I did not forget to add that, apart from the United States and Canada, all member countries were European.

The Minister had no objections, but wanted to know more. He asked me about the attitude of neighboring countries and added that he would consult with them. I gathered that Oman would join only after Saudi Arabia, and that this was an important factor to bear in mind.

He added that they had a satisfactory defense treaty with the United Kingdom and close ties with the US. In conclusion, the Sultanate was interested in this enlargement of the security area in the Middle East, but it would only join after a careful analysis of the initiative's merits.

He explained that the geostrategic position of Oman was of vital importance. The geography and navigability of the waters make it obligatory for oil tankers passing the Strait of Hormuz to transit Omani territorial waters. If, as a result of an accident or terrorist act, a ship sank, vital traffic for the rest of the world would be blocked, with unimaginable repercussions on world financial markets, not to speak of the political consequences.

A guarantee that the Strait would be kept open for navigation was therefore an acknowledged priority. This may well explain why Muscat maintains good political relations with the Iranian ayatollahs, who are just across the Strait. This point was clearly highlighted for me, in addition to the fact that Oman had no territorial disputes with other countries. The impression that the government sought to give to the outside world was that it had no outstanding tensions and was extremely comfortable in its regional context. Even the echoes of bloody acts of terrorism in Iraq seemed distant, and of little significance, there.

The Omani Parliament was a recent innovation, I tried to arrange a meeting with the President of the Parliament. However, I was informed that he did not yet feel competent to have official talks with foreign guests.

I found Oman attractive, perhaps because of its ancient history, perhaps for its architecture, colors, and its people. It is a place I would happily go back to. I purchased a map of possible mountain excursions in the vicinity of the capital. I kept it, not because I thought I really would ever go hiking there, but as a springboard for imagining mysterious summits, unexpected valleys, hidden waters, and discovering a way of life different from my own.

Upon arriving at the protocol lounge, in an airport that was devoid of any concessions to luxury and slightly retro, I concluded that it would take a long time for the country to change. In actual fact, though, following the Jasmine Revolution in Tunisia, even the roads of Muscat filled with young demonstrators. Not surprising, given that the reasons for discontent are generally similar across the greater Arab world. Still, after the promise of reforms in Oman, silence seems to have fallen, at least for the moment, though we do not know what waits around the corner in that country.

The Strait of Hormuz, though, is often in the news, with the Iranians periodically threatening to block transit, as leverage against international sanctions. The American response is characteristically immediate, making it quite clear that the Fifth Fleet would not just sit and watch from its base in Bahrain.

Before leaving Oman, I went for a walk at sunset along the shore of the Indian Ocean, where I enjoyed watching the arrival of a swarm of old boats returning from their daily fishing expedition. However, I was somewhat taken aback to see the way their catch was landed. The boats tipped the nets containing their catch onto small, rust-stained trucks, which, to facilitate this operation, had two wheels in the water. Inevitably, some of the fish fell onto the sand. The trucks headed off to the city, totally unconcerned about this loss.

In an unplanned act of piety, my bodyguard, a gigantic Flemish policeman, and I set about picking up and throwing all the fish we could gather straight back into the ocean. So saving many lives ...

The Hashemite Dynasty Rules Over a Country Seething with Problems

I needed to return to Jordan, a key country in the region mid-way between the Mediterranean and the Gulf, but with a heavy concentration of Middle Eastern problems.

An opportunity arose in the spring of 2006, when Minister of Foreign Affairs Abdel Ilah Al-Khatib organized an international conference on "NATO's aims and actions for the Mediterranean Dialogue and the broader Middle East Region" in Amman. I was invited to be the keynote speaker. (In 2011, Al-Khatib would be appointed Special Representative of the UN Secretary General for Libya.)

I remember that visit very well, in part because the 2006 World Cup Soccer Championship was in full swing. Rushing back to the Hotel Intercontinental between one appointment and the next, I managed to catch glimpses of the games that were completely enthralling Amman's ex-pat community. It was there that Hans-Christian von Reibniz, the young German diplomat who accompanied me, persuaded me go to Berlin to watch the final.

On this trip again, I had an excellent impression of Jordan. Although small and virtually without natural resources, it is respected by everyone and conducts an intelligent foreign policy. The Hashemite dynasty, originally from Mecca, knows how to move with skill, and remains in power despite living on powder keg.

Jordan has organized major international meetings and boasts a governing class above the regional average. It is noteworthy that this country manages to survive economically despite not being an energy producer and its resulting exposure to fluctuations in international prices.

Obviously, by Western standards, it is not really democratic, and indeed no one expects it to be. It is clear that, if there were truly free elections, the moderate and pro-Western line of King Abdullah II would be replaced by a more radical one. However, in some way, Jordan manages to respect the norms.

Prime Minister Marouf Al-Bakhit received me in an elegant office, completely devoid, however, of any pretense of grandeur. He spoke in pragmatic terms, and clearly expressed his intention to strengthen the political-military relationship with the Alliance. He said it was in the Jordanian national interest, since the fight against terrorism, border security, information exchange, concerted action on weapons of mass destruction, etc. were natural areas for cooperation.

I also visited the Jordanian Parliament and discussed international strategies with the chairs of various parliamentary commissions, who seemed to be very interested as well as knowledgeable on the subject.

My conversation with the Military Director of the Royal Household, an influential person who does not normally meet with foreign guests, also proved most interesting. He was rather critical of the modest concrete proposals offered by Brussels, citing, as examples, programs at the NATO Defense College and schools for higher military training. He was absolutely right. It is difficult to achieve the desired degree of friendship unless efforts are made to meet the demands of partners in a spirit of openness. I tried to make this clear in Brussels, but in most cases with little success.

Western institutions often have a sense of self-satisfied superiority that keeps us feeling authoritative, even when we fail to offer much, and fail to recognize the disappointed expectations of our interlocutors. For this reason, we do not understand the delusion that we create in our interlocutors. This was true, for example, in Pakistan: on one hand, we sought to have close ties with the leadership of the country, and on the other, we had difficulty in offering concrete support.

Our frequent lack of generosity and vision can cost us dearly. Today, Jordan is like a pressure cooker in which water is boiling. Everyone is now asking what will happen if the lid flies off, because, if it does, there will be very serious repercussions for regional stability.

Up to now, the King has managed to deflect public protest by frequently changing prime ministers or the composition of governments, and by securing economic aid from friendly countries. However, even for him, the political environment is becoming increasingly complicated, including in his traditionally loyal Bedouin tribal base. Clearly, this game of changing governments cannot go on forever.

The NATO Secretary General had asked me to find out whether the King might offer facilities for the Middle East "Training Center" that Washington had recently proposed. This was a controversial issue because, in the poisoned climate of Iraqi instability, its purpose was not clear.

The Jordanian ambassador in Brussels, Ahmad Masa'adeh, a good personal friend and a distinguished diplomat, made it clear to me that his government was basically in favor of this idea, to maintain good relations with Washington. However, in the end they did not make the offer, because Amman realized that it was walking on dangerous ground.

In 2010, Masa'adeh would become the first Secretary General of the Union for the Mediterranean. a now largely forgotten body intended to promote cooperation between the European Union and a group of Mediterranean countries, the brainchild of then French president Nicolas Sarkozy. However, Masa'adeh stepped down a year later, in protest at the lack of concrete interest on the part of governments. Another example of the stormy nature of Euro-Mediterranean politics, exemplified also by the collapse of the EU's much-touted Barcelona Process.

How Can We Get Along if We Speak Different Languages?

There is an enormous difference between the Middle East and the West, not only in terms of history and culture, but also many other things. Threat perception certainly is very different. The priority for national defense systems in these countries more often than not is internal. Although they consume a great deal of resources, these systems generally are not very modern. This is true also for the national security and intelligence services. They are instruments for the use of those in power, and the control of which may well be in the hands of members of the ruling families, whose loyalty can be counted on.

Even words that seem clear, such as strategy, information, or security, often have different meanings. Try to imagine the difficulties involved in working out common concepts. I was glad when I learned that, during the Cold War, we had seen the need to codify a certain number of words with the Soviets, to avoid misunderstandings in the use of terminology that could have resulted in serious consequences.

I had found a message that I thought would be clear to everyone: we needed to arrive at an "interoperability of human minds." The concept derives from interoperability, a military term which means the ability to conduct joint operations with the armed forces of other nations. The ability to reason with people across lines of "diversity" is admittedly somewhat different, but this new term conveys the idea.

In order to achieve this, you must create a critical mass of common activities, a nexus of interests and relationships, which becomes attractive to all. In sum, you must develop a network of nations that have the prospect of thinking alike on a number of important issues. Fortunately, NATO Secretary General Jaap de Hoop Scheffer, an outstanding diplomat and good negotiator, had given me carte blanche on this, and seemed pleased with the results obtained.

The ambassadors of member states all wanted to play with this new political toy. They began by forming a group of "like-minded" countries from Southern Europe, which considered themselves the most qualified to lead the way. However, I did not want them to form a kind of "Club Med," which was not at all the objective.

Therefore, I carefully cultivated relations with the Northern European countries, and invited them to actively support relations with the Mediterranean and the Gulf. This was something that could be advantageous for everyone. For example, thanks to project financing in Jordan, Norwegian ambassador to NATO Kai Eide, later the UN representative in Kabul, received visibility that Norway otherwise never would have had.

At a certain point, the idea took hold among the NATO permanent representatives that there was a need for greater political visibility. For this reason, work began on a "Declaration" with a capital "D," to be signed with the new partners. This was not in itself a bad idea. However, it inevitably created a link with the big unresolved problems in the region, in which we could not intervene. This was why I sought to delay this declaration as long as possible. What was the sense in spending days negotiating every word in a text that might have to be renegotiated every time something changed in the political situation? Something that can easily happen.

Numerous initiatives launched with great ambitions have failed precisely because they have suffered from the repercussions of Middle Eastern politics. The European Union's Barcelona Process, launched in 1995, a precursor to the aforementioned Union for the Mediterranean, intended to promote partnership between the European Union and the Mediterranean countries, was an example. In these situations, one government or another would block the process in retaliation for some event or another. Then there was absolutely nothing to be done.

The issue of the "Declaration" dragged on, with highs and lows, until 2006, when the Lebanese War broke out. At that point, the declaration's supporters realized that it was best to abandon such a clearly unattainable goal.

You have a better chance of success focusing on joint projects, creating a "closeness" that in time can influence the political process. In other words, a bottom-up approach. In sum, the best way to proceed is to meet frequently and to do things of common interest together, cultivating projects that grow from the bottom, rather than looking for non-existent shortcuts at the top.

It was for these reasons that I sought to maximize the possibilities for meetings and missions in the region, and to create permanent links with the nerve centers of NATO's planning and operations. The chiefs of staff of new partner countries, for example, are now regularly invited to Brussels for semi-annual meetings with NATO counterparts. Clearly this is no simple exercise. Nevertheless, it is a good step forward for military leaders to exchange views on sensitive issues and overcome historical traditions of mutual distrust.

The United Arab Emirates even decided to open an embassy to NATO. I was pleased to think of my good friend Ambassador Mohammed Salem Al-Suweidi sharing a restaurant and perhaps a barber with Canadian, Polish, and other representatives at NATO Headquarters.

How to Make Progress Despite Differences

Issues arising from the diversity of our interlocutors and the complexity of management were not easy to control. A frequently recurring problem was how to take account of the differences between Mediterranean and Gulf countries. The Maghreb ambassadors wanted to meet separately from their colleagues. They made it clear that they had different historical backgrounds, different national security challenges, and more modest economic resources than the Gulf states.

On the other hand, the Gulf ambassadors recognized differences in the threats their region faced, as compared to the Maghreb. Discussions together with Egypt, Jordan, Tunisia, Algeria, Morocco and Mauritania were cumbersome. This was quite understandable. Given my role in seeking to create personal relationships of trust with everyone and my charge to be credible in resolving problems, I was the recipient of suggestions on these issues.

A problem, however, lay in the US position, as expressed by their ambassador to NATO, Victoria Nuland, later spokesperson for Secretary of State Hillary Clinton. She had replaced Nick Burns, who had become the State Department's number three under Secretary of State Condoleezza Rice. Nuland, a career diplomat, came to NATO after serving as an advisor to Vice President Dick Cheney. She was considered connected to neo-conservative circles through her husband, Robert Kagan, a well-known foreign policy commentator.

Washington believed in putting all the Arabs together, i.e. from both the Mediterranean and Gulf countries. Across the Atlantic, they seemed to have some difficulty understanding the subtleties of relations between the two groups. Once, after a working lunch at Nuland's residence to which everyone was invited, I received protests from several ambassadors over this overly inclusive approach. I was forced therefore to ask her, in private, not to repeat meetings in that format, at the risk of undermining the political framework.

On the other side of the Middle Eastern political spectrum was Israel, where Avigdor Lieberman, a leading right-wing figure, had replaced Tzipi Livni at the Ministry of Foreign Affairs. One day he invited me to lunch at an elegant restaurant in Brussels, where we had a very civil conversation. He told me that he wanted to test the waters for an eventual availability of NATO to play an active role in Gaza. Something that was obviously impossible.

We wanted to maintain a balance between official contacts and the joint events which by now had become routine. There was no longer the problem of securing an adequate reception, and meetings with ministers were becoming more frank and directed at getting results. I remember one particular visit to Tunisia in the spring of 2007.

The purpose of the visit was a conference and a meeting with Tunisia's Minister of Defense Kamel Morjane, with whom we cordially discussed joint activities that needed to be strengthened. He also presented me with a beautiful book on Italian painters in Tunisia.

The "in" topic of conversation was newly-elected French President Nicolas Sarkozy's proclaimed intention of launching a plan for the Mediterranean, centered on the Maghreb, the region preferred by French diplomacy because of Paris's historic connection. My hosts were skeptical about the intentions behind the Union for the Mediterranean. The reaction was along the lines of "we already gave at the office." The weight given to conspiracy theories also should not be overlooked. The main topic of conversation in Sidi Bou Said restaurants was whether Sarkozy was of Jewish origin and, if so, the possible consequences. I was surprised that such an issue was regarded as so important. Once you were outside government circles, you could immediately sense prejudice towards the West, even in moderate Tunisia.

I also recall the initial coldness in our relations with Morocco, and the anxiety in the air during our initial meetings. However, the situation has gradually improved. When I met again with Youssef Amrani, Secretary General of the Ministry of Foreign Affairs in Rabat when I first visited, he amicably reminded me how together we had organized the first Atlantic Council meeting outside Europe in his country, highlighting the excellent relations we now enjoyed. This able diplomat and politician became Secretary General of the Union for the Mediterranean in the summer of 2011 and subsequently Morocco's Minister Delegate for Foreign Affairs and Cooperation, and then senior advisor to the King of Morocco.

Algeria too was giving increasing importance to its political-military cooperation with NATO. It had also drawn closer to the United States, so much so that Secretary of Defense Donald Rumsfeld paid a visit to Algiers in 2006. Unlike the Moroccans or Jordanians, however, a periodic problem with the Algerians was getting them to sit down at the same table, at a political level, with Israeli representatives.

Then there was the rivalry for regional primacy, the closing of the Moroccan-Algerian border, Jordan's strategic position between the Mediterranean and the Gulf, and Egypt's ambitions to be the "star." In short, this group was far from easy to deal with.

A good example of such complexities was the center for air traffic to and from Afghanistan in Qatar. In Doha, it was accepted that the NATO member country personnel stationed in the country would rotate and would enjoy fiscal privileges. The only condition was that, in the event of criminal acts, the people involved would not be exempt from local jurisdiction. However, NATO member countries insisted on total exemption, arguing that no one should be subject to Qatari law.

I was sent to Doha to discuss this with the government. I met with Minister for Foreign Affairs Ahmad Abdullah Al-Mahmoud, who told me clearly that it would be impossible to make a law exempting foreigners from criminal responsibility. The Emir could not expose himself to the inevitable criticisms that would follow such a clearly arbitrary public act. At the same time, he assured me that the authorities would be highly flexible in order to avoid embarrassing cases. He told us: "We will not put you in any difficulty, but we cannot write it down in a law." While cooperation and exchanges of personnel among NATO countries are governed by status of forces agreements that, among other thing, grant primary legal jurisdiction to the "sending state," one can understand how new partners might find such ideas unfamiliar and difficult to accept. He was right to ask how an independent country could decree the impunity of a foreigner.

However, in dealing with Qatar, the jurists of NATO member countries maintained their position of principle, with the result that a NATO-Qatar agreement has never been reached. The US, on the other hand, has long had its own classified bilateral defense cooperation agreement with Qatar. Here, the hoped for "interoperability of minds" between NATO and partner countries really did not work as intended.

The International Staff

The activities described in this book were organized by NATO's International Staff. There is always a degree of friction in any multinational organizations worth its salt. National delegates view themselves as the owners, and view the staff officials as a kind of foreign legion, to whom they can turn when things become complicated, but who should always be kept on a short leash. For their part, staff officials believe that, given their technical ability and the fact that they are the historical memory of the organization, they are the only ones who know how to do things. Member countries are viewed as bunglers who spend too much time quibbling among themselves and creating unnecessary problems.

I confess that my heart is on the side of international civil servants, people who have chosen a life as a sort of stateless persons in the service of an unusual business. About thirty nationalities were represented in Brussels in my time and worked rather well with one another.

Although this is perhaps a romantic vision, it seems to me that these people, together with their families, facilitate empathy among different peoples and languages and are symbolic of a greater world. Although by necessity holding a national passport, it is also wonderful to feel a little like a citizen of the world and to love this diversity. This is a growing tribe in many different professions: diplomats, military personnel, bankers, hotel workers, builders, offshore companies, etc. They are a small minority, but who knows, perhaps they are making converts for better understanding.

The Delights of Political Meetings

The political level of the emerging partnerships now needed to be revamped. That meant holding meetings of ministers of foreign affairs and defense that would also be attended by our new friends. This also meant bringing together, for the first time, governments and people who were not only different from each other, but whose objectives only to a limited extent were similar. The most difficult problem was the presence of Israeli and Arab ministers around the same table. Would it be possible for them to forget their differences for a few hours, seeing themselves as participants in joint projects?

This was a difficult enterprise, given that it needed to be accepted by all parties. Then it was necessary to agree on an agenda that was serious, but at the same time not too problematic, so as to avoid controversies that would have jeopardized the whole exercise. We all knew we were dealing with difficult interlocutors, more used to antagonism than to seeking conciliation.

A meeting of NATO defense ministers had been planned for February 2006 in Taormina, Sicily, a true symbol of the Mediterranean, which seemed the right place to invite Arabs and Israelis. Behind the scenes I worked on persuading all to attend. The Poles, Baltic nations, and other East Europeans were in fact the most reticent. The last echoes of the Cold War seemingly had just died away, but they feared a revival of Russian nationalism. This was their priority, perhaps not unjustified in light of more recent Russian actions.

Even some of the larger nations were hesitant to commit to this new path of multilateral diplomacy. Telling a white lie, I tried to reassure everyone that it was worth making the effort, and that in the end everything would go smoothly.

Once I had obtained the general consensus of all the NATO members, I began promoting the initiative externally, to ascertain whether or not it would be successful. At the end of a long round of consultations, the seven partner countries invited all accepted, but naturally each in their own way.

When I consulted Oded Eran, he immediately told me that the Israeli minister would not miss the opportunity to attack Hamas and its encouragement of terrorism. I explained to him that, in this case, it would be better if the ministers did not meet. It was better that they not see each other than to have an argument in front of the television cameras. He said that he would speak about this again in Jerusalem. From their point of view, it was positive to meet at a political level with governments that did not recognize Israel. Nevertheless, they were tempted to use the occasion to argue about terrorism.

The Algerians were grumpy and unhappy about the presence of Israel, with whom they had no wish to have political relations. As usual, the Egyptians kept their cards close to their chest about what they would eventually say or do. If, during the meeting, there were a "provocation" by anyone, the reactions of those present would be uncontrollable. If this happened, the first ever NATO meeting with the defense ministers of these countries would be a catastrophic failure.

The day before this meeting, when everything seemed to be going as planned and an agenda based on future cooperation had been agreed upon, the scandal about cartoons depicting the Prophet erupted. The Danish newspaper *Jyllands-Posten* had published a series of derisive drawings of Mohammed, which, for Muslims, was totally unacceptable.

This was more than sufficient to ignite the streets of the whole Muslim world, a reaction that was impossible to manage. An unfortunate side effect was that the Saudi government decided not to join our partnership, which it had seemed about to announce.

In addition, Danish Prime Minister Anders Fogh Rasmussen refused to condemn the author of these cartoon drawings, pointing out the right to the free expression of opinion. This made him unpopular in the Muslim world and when, in 2008, he became a candidate for NATO Secretary General, Turkey objected right to the bitter end, only standing down as a result of repeated pressure from President Obama.

Many NATO countries expressed their solidarity with Denmark, to underline that the freedom of the press was sacrosanct. It was necessary to explain to them that the defense ministers meeting was not the place for this discussion, and that statements of this kind would force the Arab ministers to react, thereby giving way to useless and damaging debates.

On the flip side of the coin, in the Muslim countries, it was expected that their ministers would express indignation for the insult to the Prophet. I had to break my neck to dissuade them from doing so. My argument was similar to the one I had used with the Israelis, when insisting that it was not advisable to make public polemical statements against Hamas.

It would have sufficed for just one of the participants to get out of line and provoke an endless debate. Fortunately, the Secretary General publically supported my position. In the end, common sense won out. The atmosphere in Taormina was highly productive, with mutual agreement that it was necessary to deepen this newborn cooperation in the field of defense and security, all recognizing their common interest in doing so. This was a good example of how the partnership was not a simple exercise, and could succeed only if given the proper care and attention.

Until the structure fully achieves its own equilibrium and can stand on its own two feet, it will require constant reconfirmation. The drive towards cohesion must overcome the temptation of isolation, which resurfaces at every step along the way. Spain sought to acquire visibility by insisting and indeed succeeding in having the ministerial meeting repeated the following year in Seville. My own hope was that the meeting would give an added impetus to the partnership process. However, as the saying goes, you can't win them all. The ministers, to be sure, expressed support for partnership, but the meeting took place with little warmth and did not provide much new energy.

A curious episode occurred. The Mauritanian ministerial delegation, which we knew for certain had disembarked at the airport, never showed up for the meeting. It remains a complete mystery how they spent the day. A somewhat surreal observation came from Afghan Minister of Defense Abdul Rahim Wardak. During the gala dinner, he maintained that the best red wine vines in the world originated in his country.

It was not possible to leave the management of this process solely in the hands of the defense ministers. Consequently, between 2004 and 2007, the foreign affairs ministers met three times, as guests of the Belgian government, at the Egmont Palace in Brussels, a majestic 16th-century building that the Ministry of Foreign Affairs now uses primarily as a conference center. Despite the normal anxieties during preparations, these meetings were conducted in a positive and constructive atmosphere, thanks notably to the NATO Secretary General's support for my efforts. Increasingly, the partnership was looking like a win, at no real cost to the Alliance.

Still, the decisions taken there had to be considered in light of diverging NATO priorities, including initiatives vis-à-vis Eastern Europe, the Caucasus, and Central Asia. Polish Ambassador Jerzy Nowak made it quite clear to me that the limit to his country's Middle Eastern cooperation would be when it involved reduced resources and attention for Eastern Europe. He need not have worried. I truly had to sweat before securing two Middle East experts for the NATO International Staff. Interestingly, the representatives of the Baltic republics were not visibly anxious about the resource implications of NATO partnerships in the Middle East.

Another problem was that, every time, those invited needed to make it clear they would accept the official invitation before the invitation was actually issued. This required zigzagging in and out between intifadas, unexpected crises, periodic bad moods, and sensational attacks. Finally, it was necessary to pilot the discussions, preventing them from touching upon big-picture controversial topics, in order to talk about the concrete cooperation and the political and practical added value that the partnership could offer. Navigating towards a shared vision and a NATO link with the Middle Eastern world required avoiding pitfalls at every step. My consolation in those years was that everyone seemed to recognize that progress was being made.

Impossible Iraq

The situation in Iraq went from bad to worse. Not a day went by without Iraqi towns and cities being shaken by bloody attacks, a cocktail of ethnic feuds and open war against the occupier. The Americans were unable to control the situation, and were forced to stay within a "Green Zone" that contained their embassy, the military high commands, and Iraqi government headquarters. The latter being periodically decimated by attacks on its ministers. Not to mention the frequent kidnappings of foreigners, which every time provoked excruciating debates, including about the conditions for their release.

US prestige in the Middle East was then at its lowest point. The flag that was initially raised to bring democracy to the Middle East gradually fell into tatters and lost its color.

I often travelled to the region, and my interlocutors there were critical of Washington, which they said kept making one error after another. They considered the situation a disaster from the start, but were slow to say so openly, since their interests lay in maintaining close ties with the United States. No one had a clear idea how it all would end and what the consequences would be for their respective countries.

Neighboring Kuwait was worried. I well recall Sheikh Thamer Al-Ali Al-Sabah, president of the National Security Bureau, complaining about the invasion's long-term results, even though Kuwait owed its survival to the Americans who had gone to war to free them from Saddam Hussein's occupation.

Now, in private, they criticized Iraqi Prime Minister Nouri al-Maliki, saying he was an improvised statesman in a role beyond his capabilities. The Kuwaitis were saying that the political movements that were springing up in Iraq had unclear origins and objectives. In the background, there was a steady stream of reciprocal ethnic cleansing wherever there was a Sunni or Shiite minority.

Fortunately, NATO was mostly outside all of this. Its only involvement in Iraq was some training, including running the Joint Staff College, a training center at Ar-Rustimaya, historic site of the Iraqi Military Academy, where, despite numerous problems, training courses were held for future senior officers of the Iraqi armed forces. This was a small, but necessary, price for solidarity with the US.

In September 2005, NATO Secretary General Jaap de Hoop Scheffer made a visit to open the academy. He told me that the US Air Force plane carrying him and top US military leaders had barely taken off from Baghdad when the pilot asked them to stand up immediately and look out the windows at the ground below. He asked them if they could make out any armed men or signs of missiles, so that he could quickly maneuver to avoid them. The fear only ended after leaving Iraqi airspace. This episode speaks for itself, since it was not possible to ensure security even at Baghdad's airport.

Iraq was going up in flames, and the US military already had had more than four thousand casualties. Americans who served there understandably speak of it as a very negative experience.

The situation improved in 2007 when US General David Petraeus pursued an intelligent policy of rapprochement with the Sunni insurgency and convinced Washington to send additional troops. This phase is referred to as the "surge." On August 31, 2010 President Barack Obama declared the end of the Operation Iraqi Freedom and the last American soldier left the country in December 2011.

It is disconcerting to think that the stated goal at that historic time was democratization of the Arab world. However, in this there were elements of sincerity, as well as of simplistic thinking. In his memoirs, for example, former UK prime minister Tony Blair speaks of George W. Bush as an American president with a highly simplistic vision of the world. There are accounts of conversations with President Bush in which he expressed surprise that the Sunni insurgency appeared to be resistant to any attempt at conciliation. "Why don't they seek a simpler and more active everyday life, like we do here in America?" he is quoted as saying.

The future of Iraq remains uncertain. On one hand, it has still not digested the trauma of the civil war and the reversal of the power structure that brought the Shiites to power. On the other hand, Iraq became the first Arab government in the modern era with popular representation, an elected parliament in which diverse political forces jostled. It is yet to be seen how it will withstand the tests that lie ahead, including the existence of a Kurdish quasi-state in the north that is, not surprisingly, resistant to sharing its petroleum revenues with the rest of the country.

In addition, there is the strong Iranian influence about which volumes have been written. Nevertheless, the historic divide between Arabs and Persians has never ceased to exist. Therefore, there is no guarantee that a shared Shiite creed will continue to be as important as it is today.

It is to be sincerely hoped that Iraq returns to its natural historic state. We must remember that the Tigris and Euphrates basin, ancient Mesopotamia, was the very cradle of civilization.

The Green Olive Trees of Tel Aviv

In November 2005, the tenth anniversary of Yitzhak Rabin's assassination was solemnly commemorated in the Knesset and in highly symbolic places such as Mount Herzl, Israel's national cemetery. The international delegations were guests at the King David Hotel. Also there was Igor Ivanov, the former Russian minister of foreign affairs and then secretary of the National Security Council at the Kremlin. I told him that there was no way I could have missed him, as my car was always right behind his in the motorcade. Laughing, he said that, for once, it was NATO following Russia and not the other way around. Another noteworthy guest was German Minister of Foreign Affairs Joschka Fischer, admired for his innovative ideas, but, according to rumor, detested by his coworkers, whom he arrogantly treated in a condescending manner. His aide, a female German diplomat, maintained an enigmatic demeanor. At a certain point, we found ourselves together on the hotel terrace, enjoying the amazing view.

Taking advantage of this opportunity, the Israeli Ministry of Foreign Affairs organized a working dinner at the King David Hotel. The partnership was no longer a mysterious object, but rather a source of added value that should be discussed.

In order to avoid any misunderstanding, I always explained that our policy was to give all the Mediterranean Dialogue countries the same opportunities. Although Israel could profit the most, it should never be thought that NATO had a preferential channel with Jerusalem, otherwise the whole structure could easily collapse.

I was taken to a small airport on the Mediterranean from where drones were taking off. It was quite a spectacle to see these small aircraft take off with the blue sky in the background. Drones are highly useful in the surveillance of hostile territory, and carry the most sophisticated photography and film equipment available. They are of immense value to Israel for acquiring information and for decision making in the field. I saw some images in which it was even possible to pick out the registration number of a motorbike carrying two Hezbollah operatives in southern Lebanon on their way to a makeshift rocket launch site.

Until then Israel had substantially been in a winning position. However, the illusion of near invulnerability is dangerous, because in the long term strategic balances can change. The regime change in Egypt some years later took Israel by surprise. The Arab Spring temporarily put Israel on the defensive, and the government appeared to be short of political options. However, the 2013 military overthrow of Mohamed Morsi, the Egyptian president elected from the ranks of the Muslim Brotherhood, seems to have put Egyptian-Israeli relations back on track.

Another challenge for Israel, of course, are the potential long-term effects on Israeli society of conflict with the Palestinians. The former Minister of Foreign Affairs Tzipi Livni recently wrote that Israel's pride in being the only democracy in the Middle East would cease to exist when democracy came to an end on the virtual border with the Palestinians, which Israel refused to acknowledge.

In Jerusalem, I went to visit the Church of the Holy Sepulchre. Inside, I briefly spoke to the long-bearded Greek Orthodox monk who oversaw the entry of the faithful. Showing a surprising and unexpected knowledge of the subject, he rattled off from memory the composition of Inter Milan's soccer team for the previous 20 years.

At the end of the visit, I attended a large official dinner in Tel Aviv for the inauguration of the Yitzhak Rabin Center, a museum and center for promoting historical knowledge: a beautiful place, modern, sunny, and surrounded by majestic olive trees. On that occasion, I was able to see for myself the close ties between Israel and the Jewish community in the United States. Important members of that community were present, and the Center continues to receive significant private financial support from the US. The Clintons were also present, a further indication of very high-level connections between the two countries.

Hillary Clinton made a speech in which she hinted at her presidential ambitions, then Bill Clinton spoke. He was still a great orator, able to ignite hearts, a true politician of the first order, while the future secretary of state was technically perfect, but with little charisma.

I was at table with Rabin's former chief of staff. Listening to the speeches in remembrance of the Prime Minister, he told me that Rabin, to whom he referred as "Yitzhak," was a simple person. If he had been able to attend, he would have been taken aback at all the merits being attributed to him.

One Does Not Speak
If the King Does Not Ask

Everything indicated that the times were changing fast, and that it was necessary to make people understand this. There was no government in the region that did not suggest a media push towards the Arab public as a priority.

The West was beginning to realize that it had to improve relations with this part of the world, getting to know one another better, and reassuring the Arabs of respect for their sovereignty and the absence of any hidden Western designs. NATO wanted to be recognized as a friendly political organization, and not simply a military instrument. So, at a certain point it was necessary to make a decision on the best strategy to follow. However, the task that had to be tackled was one of the most difficult, because deep-rooted perceptions needed to be changed. What was to be done?

Clearly not just one thing. The first decision, which upset the European research institutes, was to move all planned meetings, seminars, symposia, and such to Arab territory. Carrying out public activities in North Africa or in the Middle East, with the use of local media, would enable us to address a larger public, and facilitate wider diffusion of our message. There was another issue. Up until that point, high-level meetings had always been held on European soil. This clearly did not appear to be in line with the two-way street that we had declared to be indispensable.

It was therefore necessary to come up with an idea for a high visibility political event in an Arab country that would attract media attention. My preference was to start with a country on the southern shores of the Mediterranean, since it would be better understood by everyone. The Gulf could follow later.

While we were testing the waters with Arab representatives, Morocco agreed to host an official meeting of the North Atlantic Council and Mediterranean Dialogue country representatives in Rabat. That an Arab government for the first time took responsibility for such a dialogue with NATO on its own territory was a positive step. From our point of view, it was useful in showing that decisions were made by consensus. In other words, the Alliance was not simply a tool in the hands of the US. Also, in strategic dialogue, NATO's primary function was political rather than military.

The result was that the North Atlantic Council (at the level of permanent representatives) would meet for the first time on another continent. Step by step, an important objective was becoming reality. This involved diplomatic activity at various levels, coordination among those involved, dinners at the Moroccan ambassador's residence, etc.

The Moroccan government proposed a date in April 2006 and a suitable agenda for a serious exchange of opinions. I presided over the meeting, which was attended by all the Alliance ambassadors, as well as those of the Arab partner nations.

Upon arrival in Rabat, however, I did receive a shock. Youssef Amrani, at that point Director General for Bilateral Relations at the Moroccan Ministry of Foreign Affairs, subsequently (as of 2012) Minister Delegate for Foreign Affairs and Cooperation in the Moroccan government, and currently senior advisor to the King of Morocco, arrived at the airport with the proposed text of a political document to be approved that very day by the meeting participants. In and of itself, the document was acceptable, if perhaps somewhat ingenuous. However, it was difficult to imagine how so many countries gathered together in Rabat could unanimously approve a declaration they had not known about previously, and which they would not have time to clear with their capitals.

I managed to convince Youssef, a clever and distinguished person, to abandon the idea, explaining to him that approval of a political text was one of the most sensitive exercises in multinational settings. I understood the visibility that Rabat wanted to obtain from the initiative, but discussion about the document might have ruined the conference and achieved the exact opposite of the intended result.

Having dealt with this issue, the atmosphere turned out to be better than expected. Everyone understood the important symbolism of a North Atlantic Council meeting held for the first time in North Africa, with Arab countries participating in the full light of day, along with Israel. The speeches were all positive in tone, urging enhanced cooperation. And all the participants got along well. Political-military cooperation with the southern shores of the Mediterranean was beginning to appear tangible. But the discussions only could go so far. We had to maintain a sort of constructive, yet fragile ambiguity, and somehow managed to strike the right balance.

Local media coverage added a seal of approval to the meeting. As chair of the meeting, I held a press conference, with a good media turnout and plenty of visible interest. Previously, we had had cordial meetings with governments, and then discovered that the public knew nothing about them. The Moroccan government, on the other hand, showed considerable courage in publicizing the event as much as they did.

In Rabat, we were surrounded by lush greenery, flowers, and water. The city's beauty seemed in itself a sign of opening towards the outside world and of its ancient ways of life. I had the impression that the air in Morocco was denser, heavier with a more powerful scent than that in Italy, giving a sensation of special vitality.

At the end of the conference, I was received by Prince Moulay Rachid, second in line to the throne, in an elegant pavilion before a sumptuously laden table. The prince was young, in his 30s, and wore an elegant pinstriped suit.

This was an unprecedented gesture of courtesy. We had a very formal conversation, with the customary questions and answers on international strategy and its prospects, and naturally the international position and role of Morocco. The ministers of defense and interior were present at the meeting, but to my great surprise did not utter a single word.

It was explained to me that in these cases the rules of protocol dictate that they could only speak if requested to do so by the King or the person in line for the throne. A detail that helps one understand the traditions and the remoteness of the royal family.

The sovereign has a religious mantle as well, deriving from

the fact that he is a direct descendant of the Prophet, through his daughter Fatima. The King can therefore boast the title of Sharif. For many centuries, the names of legitimate sharifs were recorded in a kind of genealogical family tree, an immense scroll kept in Mecca.

What Comes First,
Policy or Communication?

The importance of communication is right in front of everyone's eyes. It is true that, in the end, the young demonstrators in Cairo's Tahrir Square were not the victors. However, the fact remains that those events never would have happened without the Internet, Facebook, Twitter, text messaging, and mobile phones. This has been the subject of extensive research. At a certain point, the Egyptian authorities decided to shut down the Internet for a few days, to prevent the spread of news, but by then it was too late. Given their enormous viewership, Al Arabiya and Al Jazeera also need to be added to the picture. In the world today, everyone can see everything, and this is something we have begun to understand and take seriously.

Profound change is underway everywhere. There are inevitable problems arising from the contrast between modern communication and traditional realities, which create confusion for people. However, overall, thanks to these tools of communication, consciousness about personal dignity is gaining ground. During the years described in these pages, our objective was to show that the West was changing its attitude and was capable of giving something useful to the Arabs, that interests in the political-strategic-military field could come together, and that there were also shared values.

Following the example of Rabat, a number of other high-level conferences were held. These involved the entire North Atlantic Council and leading figures from the region, who for the first time spoke in public about cooperation with the West in the sensitive area of regional security.

Progress in the relationship with the Gulf countries also was evident. The government of Kuwait and NATO co-hosted a December
2006 conference in Kuwait City on the way ahead for the Istanbul
Cooperation Initiative (ICI). Meetings of the North Atlantic Council
with the four countries fully participating in the initiative began
in Bahrain in 2008, with similar meetings in Abu Dhabi in 2009, in
Doha in 2010, and again two years later. The first such meeting at
the level of foreign ministers would take place in April 2014. The
host governments always expended vast resources on these conferences. They even sent planes to Brussels to transport the members
of the North Atlantic Council.

It was becoming increasingly clear that governments in the Gulf
were seeking added visibility and importance in the eyes of major
Western countries. They wanted recognition and consideration. It
was also a way to form friendships that would make an external
attack more difficult. Along with this was the ambition of emerging
countries to show that their future was not solely dependent on oil,
by establishing suitable relationships in other sectors.

There was even a certain rivalry among them to be "at the center of the photo." Qatar was perhaps the most dynamic. In terms of
visibility, Qatar had started later than the others, but was making
up for lost time. Because they had the necessary financial resources,
hotels, and good communications, it was easy for them to host important events and invite famous personalities. A couple of years
earlier, Stephen Larrabee of the RAND Corporation had told me
that he had been contacted by the Qataris about organizing an important event involving NATO. My friend was quite surprised that
Doha wanted contacts with an organization about which, at that
time, they still knew very little, and for which they were prepared
to allocate substantial funds.

I thought contacts with Qatar were important, and visited Doha
a number of times. On several occasions, the government proposed
hosting an international conference on cooperation with the Alliance, open to guests from the entire region. However, between 2005
and 2006, Qatar's relations with the United States deteriorated. In
Washington, Vice President Dick Cheney was especially unhappy
with the Al-Thani dynasty.

Their disagreement was about Qatari-owned Al Jazeera's political line, and the attitude of the Qatari government during its two-year term on the UN Security Council. The final straw was the gift of considerable sums of money to movements considered dangerous by the US. The American ambassador to NATO told me that this had to be borne in mind.

I discussed this unpleasant situation in Doha with Mohammed Al-Rumaihi, assistant undersecretary for "follow-up" at the Ministry of Foreign Affairs, a very competent and operational person. (He is now Minister of Municipality and Environment in the Qatari government.) He reacted saying that the Americans insisted on the introduction of multiple media outlets, but once Al Jazeera had been created, they complained about it.

Perhaps the truth lies somewhere in the middle. It is true that, during the hot years of the Iraq War, films of executions of hostages regularly were sent to Al Jazeera and often shown on air. The result was that Doha had to wait until 2010 before it could host an official conference with the Alliance. Saudi Arabia as well was engaging in a little political zigzagging at the time, but there seemed to be more leniency towards the Saudis.

By the way, for historical/dynastic reasons the emirs of Qatar do not have the best relations with Riyadh. Indeed, there have been periods when diplomatic relations have been broken. One was in 1995, when the Emir took over from his father, Khalifa bin Hamad Al-Thani, by advising him not to return from his holidays. In June 2017, Saudi Arabia led a group of Arab countries in cutting off relations with Qatar, alleging that Doha had ties to terrorist and sectarian groups seeking to destabilize the region. Some commentators suggested that the actual motivation was Saudi unhappiness with Qatar's foreign policy, which sought to balance Saudi influence with an autonomous foreign policy and reasonably good ties to Iran.

The Qatari leadership clearly has sought to establish its own distinctive profile in the Gulf region. Launching Al Jazeera International, an English-language channel managed by experienced BBC journalists, was part of this effort. Although it has come under diverse accusations of bias, the importance of Al Jazeera is hard to dispute. It certainly was an undisputed protagonist of the Arab Spring. We can all remember, for example, the TV cameras rolling for hours, filming the squares of Benghazi filled with protestors. Perhaps, it was this visibility that encouraged the international intervention in Libya, which has resulted retrospectively in so much debate.

Doha also has the ambition to become one of the major convention centers in the world, host top-level events, and attract illustrious foreign institutions. They even have built a motorcycle racetrack where the Qatar Grand Prix is held. It is one of the rounds in the world championship. The race, which I attended in the Emir's presence, takes place at night with perfect illumination.

France profited from the stalemate in Qatari-American relations by convincing the government to establish a branch of the famous Saint-Cyr French military academy. Seeking to acquire a special relationship, Paris decided to treat Qatar as its focus country in the Gulf.

In sum, communication and politics are closely intertwined. A further example comes from WikiLeaks, which, for better or worse, has acquired an authority that is difficult to demolish, and has provided us with various views on this troubled world through the diplomatic messages that have been leaked. This includes information concerning relations and the concealed disputes between Washington and Doha in the period we are discussing.

We also found out through WikiLeaks that King Abdullah of Saudi Arabia, in private, had put pressure on Washington, hoping for military intervention against Iranian nuclear sites. It is clear that a powerful Iran poses a threat to the Al Saud dynasty, as it does to the rest of the Gulf. Only the most naïve among us could be surprised to hear that those reigning in Riyadh, the aspiring capital of the Sunni world, hoped to have the nuclear capacity of the leading Shiite country crushed at birth. The King certainly did not say so out of sympathy for Tel Aviv. However, these revelations presumably were music to Israeli ears, as they seemed to legitimize a preventive attack against Tehran. (However, that prospect seems, at least for the moment, more distant since the 2015 nuclear accord with Iran.)

It is no great surprise that, contrary to their public statements, Arab rulers in private actually take the presence and influence of Israel for granted. Although Qatar, for example, does not fully recognize the State of Israel, contacts, including in the commercial realm, have been extensive. Significantly, the messages published by WikiLeaks also highlighted the weakness of the Palestinian movement and of Abu Mazen. Mossad would be tempted to say that, without Israel, Hamas already would have taken over not only Gaza but also the West Bank. A Lebanese defense minister is even reported as having given Israel suggestions on how to attack his country without hitting the Christian population, and only targeting Hezbollah. In Tunisia, cables from the American Embassy highlighted the lavish lifestyle enjoyed by President Ben Ali's family; if not the sole cause, certainly another reason for the revolution. There is no shortage of other examples.

Returning to my story, however, NATO basically tried to find the right occasions to convey public messages, and missions in the Mediterranean and Gulf regions provided good opportunities. It became my practice to give TV interviews, hold press conferences, and meet with leading figures in civil society, in addition to those in government. The local authorities considered well-balanced media coverage useful for getting public opinion accustomed to these new emerging relationships. This was a sensitive issue on the personal level, however, since I did not want the Secretary General or any NATO member countries to feel that I was going out of bounds.

For this reason, I adopted the policy of not making statements to the major international press agencies, as they could end up on peoples' desks back in Brussels and give rise to misunderstandings. In each country, I dealt only with the local media. It was not only the easiest way to handle the situation, but also did not create undesirable waves elsewhere.

In this way, I also got to know all kinds of publications and television stations that I never would have identified as important without the excellent advice I received. Like everywhere in the world, it frequently was necessary to wait for a time until the television crews had finished setting up the cables and lighting in hotel suites before I could meet with the local journalists. Overcoming some initial awkwardness, I came to see these brief TV appearances as important steps. I liked the idea of contributing to greater empathy with the Arab world.

Every now and again, though, I thought about Lord Robertson's advice to me: "Don't worry about the questions journalists ask you, usually they just try to make it difficult for you. Reply with the message you want to give, and if it has no connection with the question they ask you, don't worry about it."

It was in Bahrain in the autumn of 2007 that I gave my last interview on local TV in my NATO capacity. I told the young woman reporter that it was necessary to continue opening, one after the other, the many doors that still remained closed in the world, because everyone would benefit. The most wonderful thing to bring about would be greater understanding among civilizations that have more things in common than we often believe. The difficulty lies in having the will and the persistence to go look for common denominators and overcome the instinct for isolation.

Human Minds are Interoperable:
The NATO Defense College
Middle East Faculty

Some issues have powerful symbolism. At the end of 2005, Washington proposed opening a "Training Center" in the Middle East. This idea was not clearly defined and seemed to range from training to instruction to a sort of military academy. This issue was inevitably controversial, and the discussion that took place among the various member states was very difficult. Many asked what image the Alliance was seeking to project in Arab countries. It was easy to create misunderstandings. It could mean a school for anti-terrorist training or give the impression of being excessively military in nature. In addition, who would be willing to take on the difficult political responsibility of hosting this kind of center? In sum, what message would it send?

During a visit to Washington, a senior official responsible for Europe and NATO at the National Security Council explained to me, perhaps a little ingenuously, the desire to put mechanisms into place for increasing military capacity. In this, she was not too convincing.

Mutual interest being a fundamental principle, we asked our partners for their opinions on this. It was difficult for them to respond, because they were being pulled in various directions.

They listened carefully, but since they also did not understand what this was driving at, were somewhat non-committal. Nor did they want, quite rightly, to support an initiative on which the Alliance was internally divided.

Finally, the Jordanian government indicated that, if asked, it would provide a site. The Jordanian ambassador in Brussels, Ahmad Masa'adeh, was in a difficult position. On one hand, he was declaring his government's willingness, while, on the other hand, still waiting for the conclusion of NATO's own internal discussions. In the background was Amman's desire for visibility, as well as pressure from the United States.

Qatar, however, had already made its choice, and stepped up without any hesitation. The world as seen from Doha seemed much simpler, with fewer shades of gray. However, everyone felt it was too hasty to go directly to the Gulf.

The idea of the center was well grounded, in the sense of bringing together civilians and military from different countries on strategic issues. Not, therefore, specifically for anti-terrorism training.

I became increasingly convinced that, if the center was established as an institution "of excellence" in Europe, instead of in the Middle East, it would provide good added value, rather than becoming a problem. Furthermore, it would fill an existing gap. My research concluded by pointing toward the NATO Defense College in Rome, a unique, high-level institution with experience in hosting a wide variety of guests, while maintaining high academic standards.

After various attempts, some in private, I managed to convince the American ambassador to NATO, Victoria Nuland, that this was the best solution and would be a success. If this experiment worked, it could easily be repeated in the Middle East, but, in the meantime, the NATO Defense College solution would allow matters to mature.

At this point, I realized that it also was necessary to propose an actual model for the center. Otherwise, what would come out of negotiations among 27 countries without a clear idea? It could take years. Above all, the new center must not become a cultural ghetto. It should take in civilians and military personnel from new partners and NATO allies. They should be people with the potential for becoming leaders in their nations of origin.

Activities had to be focused on strategic issues, those at the intersection of foreign policy, security, and contemporary military skills. Given that this was an experiment, I asked Rolf Schwarz, the Arab specialist in the NATO International Staff to help me identify the best existing institutions of this kind.

In addition to the Arab ambassadors, I consulted Oded Eran

from Israel, who also held the view that it would be a good idea to launch an institution for future members of national elites.

Because of the symbolism involved, the final headache was finding a suitable name for the center. In the end, the name "Middle East Faculty" was agreed upon at the Riga Summit in late November 2006, the last one attended by George W. Bush.

Today, the creation of the Middle East Faculty at the NATO Defense College in Rome has brought together civilians and military personnel from Europe, North America, Arab countries and Israel, to address key issues and prepare the future. It is operational and I hope that it may gain high visibility, as this innovative projetc deserves.

There are few things capable of creating long-term relationships like a period of study spent together examining difficult subjects. It creates networks of people and contacts that hopefully continue to develop over time, to everybody's advantage.

I was pleased with the end result, a reward for a long task in which I had invested all my energy. There were also other tasks in those years. I regularly received parliamentary and academic delegations, especially Americans, coming to see what the Alliance was doing. At a certain point, for example, David Abshire, a leading American defense intellectual, came to Brussels. He had been close to multiple presidents since Cold War days. He was struck by the dynamic attention we were giving to the Middle East, and felt it was innovative and concrete. He told me he had had similar ideas. When I later visited him in Washington, he explained his initiative, the "Foundation for the Future," which aimed at involving Arab countries in the most advanced forms of media communication.

During the Riga Summit, I had lunch with US Secretary of State Condoleezza Rice. She told me about her typical working day, which began at six in the morning, if not earlier, and finished late at night. He life was one of great sacrifice, and she was able to stand up to enormous pressure.

I realized that, for an African-American woman from Alabama to become the Secretary of State of the United States, she had had to prove she was the best at everything. It was obvious that she had the total respect of the President, who often looked in her direction during meetings for tacit confirmation. Incidentally, contrary to how he is often portrayed, George W. Bush is not an unpleasant person.

Secretary Rice had begun her professional life as an academic expert on Soviet issues, and was known for a very critical view of the Soviet system at a time when a distinctly softer view had come to dominate in US academic circles. Her support for Ukraine, Georgia, and missile defense, which resulted in tense relations with the Russian leadership, were no surprise. She had her own strong ideas, and was not a creature of Vice President Cheney or Secretary of Defense Rumsfeld.

I had a chance, by the way, to observe Cheney at a conference in the Lithuanian capital Vilnius, where he lambasted Russia for violating democracy and human rights. The Cold War tone might have sounded good in Vilnius, but it clearly infuriated the Russian leadership.

The Egyptians Remain Doubtful

Egypt plays a key strategic role in the Middle East and, along with Saudi Arabia, is the most important country in the region. At the same time, its ambition is to maintain Egypt's position as a leader in the politics of Africa, as well as the Middle East.

In February 2006, I made a trip to Cairo to attend an Egyptian Council on Foreign Affairs conference that actually had been organized around my visit. As such events became more usual, the debate with the public became more open and questions that were closest to people's hearts began to come out. Anger about the special relationship between Washington and Israel came to light, accusations of double standards, etc. were heard. I tried my best to explain certain positions, but obviously could not deviate from policies agreed among all the NATO countries.

I met with Minister of Defense Field Marshall Mohammed Hussein Tantawi, later the provisional head of state following the fall of President Hosni Mubarak. I had met him several years previously, when Beniamino Andreatta, the Italian minister of defense, had invited him to Rome.

You could tell Tantawi's rank by the number of aides swarming around him. This man had long years of government experience behind him and could not be easily moved. Tall and slim, he had an aristocratic quality that never failed to impress me. He was a man of few words, and limited himself to saying that, in his opinion, the prospect of a military relationship with the Alliance was a good line to follow.

In 2011, Tantawi took on the heavy task of ferrying the country towards the future, seeking to maintain a privileged position for the armed forces. Since then, there have been many surprises in Egypt and more are possible. However, the fact remains that it is a traditionally moderate country, with an established intellectual elite, and will need long-term international assistance.

Following my somewhat colorless meeting with the Field Marshall, I had a significant political conversation with Minister of Foreign Affairs Ahmad Aboul Gheit, who in 2016 would become Secretary General of the Arab League. He received me in his bright, spacious office overlooking the Nile, telling me that, although he was more than happy to develop our relations, NATO had exaggerated ambitions and should be more careful about its public statements, which raised suspicion elsewhere. I asked him the reasons for this blunt criticism. He replied that, in his February speech at the annual *Wehrkunde* meeting in Munich, Secretary General de Hoop Scheffer had said that the Alliance would become the world's policeman. The *Wehrkunde* is arguably the most important annual conference on international security, and is traditionally attended by leading figures from all over the world.

I categorically denied that the Secretary General would have expressed such an idea, which was confirmed by Thomas Wagner, who had actually prepared the speech and who fortunately was present. I asked if we could reread the text together to verify the language used. De Hoop Scheffer in effect had said that the Alliance intended "to project stability" and "to expand security" in other parts of the globe. He actually intended the complete opposite of a global policeman role, proposing rather to act in cooperation with other international players and organizations, with the aim of increasing collective security.

He had indicated NATO's desire to become a factor for stability through its partnerships, the foundations for which were already being laid. This was quite different from being some kind of guarantor of world security.

This is a classic example of how words can be interpreted in a completely different way from their original intention. The meaning given to them in Cairo was partly due to conspiracy theories, and perhaps also due to a lack of knowledge concerning certain terms widely used in NATO circles.

The Minister read and reread the text several times, asking a number of questions. In the end, he concluded that I was right, and that he had received an inaccurate assessment from his staff. I was very happy to have cleared up a misunderstanding that could have produced serious consequences, if it had not been rectified in good time. It is anybody's guess how many cases like this occur every day all over the world. Accompanying me to the door, Aboul Gheit launched into an unexpected avalanche of praise for his body-guards and other support personnel from Nubia, the southernmost part of Egypt.

Later I had an amusing experience. I had a few hours free and went to visit one of Cairo's ancient mosques, together with my staff. The custodian asked my nationality, before proceeding to praise Italy for having restored the mosque's roof, which had been in a state of collapse. I then learned that the Egyptian newspapers had covered this extensively, so one could rightly say that, in that case, it was money well spent.

Back to the Gulf,
but Remember Ramadan

NATO's developing relations in the Greater Middle had to be managed on a continuous basis. Periodically it was necessary to pick up the conversation where we had left off, otherwise it might be misunderstood or ended entirely. It was therefore essential to exchange ideas with those in charge in the new partner countries.

Note that this book describes events that ended about three years before the beginning of the Arab Spring. Well before the end of my service at NATO, we were no longer in the phase of initial contact with the Middle Eastern partners. We no longer had to explain everything from the very beginning. Cooperation was underway, and the main issue under discussion was how it could best be structured and remain sustainable in the long term.

I returned many times to this special region to strengthen relations and update proposals. Among the Arabian Peninsula countries there were obvious similarities, the main one being that they all were monarchies. Still, in the countries of the Gulf region there were clear differences in style, which were easily noted when travelling from one capital to another. In the Mediterranean region, Morocco is the only country with a king. Elsewhere, royal families are just part of history.

Organizing a trip was invariably difficult, all the more so when having to go to several different places. The most important thing to know is that there are only three work days that are the same as those in Europe: Mondays, Tuesdays, and Wednesdays. On Thursdays and Fridays, they do not work, while in the West we do not work on Saturdays and Sundays. And, just to add to the confusion, in Israel Saturday is a non-working day.

In brief, welcome to the kingdom of diversity! And to confuse ideas a little more, it is also necessary to take account of Ramadan, a holy month of religious observance when the faithful fast during the day and eat only after sunset. Unlike most Western traditions, where special occasions are celebrated on set days, the dates for holidays are fixed according to the lunar calendar. Therefore, the beginning and end of Ramadan are linked to the phases of the moon and every year the dates change.

If you plan a trip to the area, as I have frequently done, it is absolutely essential to bear this in mind, as no foreign delegation will be received during Ramadan. Therefore, before setting off, I had to think carefully, so I would not find myself arriving during that special month.

Kuwait is the most northern of the Gulf countries and occupies the most sensitive position, as it neighbors Iran, Iraq, and Saudi Arabia. There is civil society in Kuwait, and a number of women hold public office. As previously mentioned, in December 2006, NATO and the Kuwaiti government sponsored a major conference, which was entitled "NATO and Gulf Countries: Facing Common Challenges through the Istanbul Cooperation Initiative." The discussion focused on the strategic situation and emerging cooperation.

Political and academic representatives were invited from neighboring countries, and maximum media visibility was assured. The event was designed as something in between a political meeting and a high-level international brainstorming session, and that mix seemed to work. The gathering was quite significant from a political point of view: Iran is a few kilometers away from Kuwait's border with Iraq, and the ayatollahs in Qom probably were wondering why the Atlantic Alliance was sticking its nose into the Shatt-el-Arab. In any case, it was easy to understand why Kuwait was so interested. For a small country surrounded by such neighbors, it was useful to display publicly the friendship of a prominent and capable organization. Increasingly we were finding that the stereotype of Arab dislike for NATO as a distinctly Western military alliance, a stereotype that the French in particularly tended to invoke, did not correspond to reality. A gradual and tempered approach, avoiding extravagant promises, in a spirit of transparency, trust, and friendship, can accomplish a great deal.

Our Kuwaiti hosts kindly organized an interesting day in the desert, which involved riding camels, watching hunting with falcons, and saber duels in the traditional style. The desert is clearly the center of local traditional culture. Every NATO permanent representative also received a computer as a gift, to the great chagrin of Her Majesty's Ambassador Peter Ricketts, subsequently National Security Adviser in the Cameron government. He explained to everyone that accepting gifts was contrary to the Foreign Office code of ethics.

In September 2007, I returned to Kuwait to meet Prime Minister Nasser Al-Sabah, an influential member of the royal family who had been head of government for many years.

He maintained that it was now necessary to go on to the next stage: the training of managers, specific projects, participation in joint exercises, and regular political meetings.

He announced that Kuwait was opening a military office in Brussels. I returned the gesture by replying that experts would be sent to his country to inform and advise on possible common projects. We were fully aware that there was still a lot to be done in the field of political consultation. I invited him to Brussels to give a presentation to the North Atlantic Council, where, as a guest, he could speak directly to the various country representatives.

Iraqi Prime Minister Ayad Allawi, predecessor to Nouri al-Maliki, already had attended a similar meeting of the Atlantic Council. I still remember that event, as I presided over the meeting, during which I unconsciously began to imagine Allawi's turbulent and adventurous past. During Saddam Hussein's regime, he had been the leading voice of Iraqis in exile. He projected authority in public.

In connection with my meeting with the Prime Minister, the Kuwait News Agency organized a round table with local analysts and journalists, giving a high profile to my visit. There was an embarrassing moment when I gave a lady journalist from a neighboring country, whom I had met on various occasions, a light kiss on the cheek, as is our custom in the West. Though without drawing back, she whispered to me: "Look, here you don't do that with an Arab woman."

Nasser Al-Sabah resigned in November 2011 when the first waves of the Arab Spring had reached the Gulf, with street protests even in Kuwait. Change in government leadership brings with it many unknowns. On one hand, it can be a sign of democratic progress, but sometimes it appears primarily as an attempt to manage situations, offering half measures rather than accepting the need for more profound political change. Controversial elections would be held in Kuwait in 2012, and again in 2013 and 2016, all of them pointing to significant, and also diverse, opposition to the status quo. You could say that clouds were beginning to appear in the clear Kuwaiti skies.

Bahrain, with which I had some familiarity, was only a short hop from Kuwait. I met first with Crown Prince Salman bin Hamad Al-Khalifa, who never missed an opportunity to reiterate his priorities: regional stability and security above all, and consequently his great hope of establishing links with the West. Moreover, even the King had expressed his desire for the presence of Alliance ships in the port of the capital, Manama.

I received a warm and unexpected thank you from the Crown Prince for the architectural work I had carried out in those years, something he repeated several times. With great courtesy, he said that there were people who were able in political and human architecture, and in opening doors.

I was pleased to be seen as an architect of good things. This was a clear sign of the Prince's personal openness and political approval. His reputation was that of a modernizer. He was dynamic and had received a Western education. It was said that, together with his counterpart in the United Arab Emirates, he would promote reforms in step with the times in the Gulf kingdoms.

In turn, the Minister of Defense and Chief of Staff, made unexpected overtures for possible contributions to Alliance operations. There was therefore no hesitation in promoting contacts at various levels, and the Training Cooperation Initiative received great support. The Bahrainis asked to attend the Special Committee meetings in Brussels where information was exchanged among the various intelligence services. From my point of view, this was a big thing and I was even a little surprised. Finally, for symbolic reasons, I was introduced to Nizar bin Sadiq Al Baharna, Minister of State for Foreign Affairs, who was a member of Bahrain's majoritarian but politically underrepresented Shiite community.

I also visited the brand-new Formula One racetrack. The director, a young British manager who appeared as if he had just stepped out of the *Financial Times* weekend supplement, explained the project in great detail. While he was giving an impeccable briefing, I could not help but wonder about his possible salary.

During those years, generally in airports, I often happened to meet John Chipman, director of the International Institute for Strategic Studies in London. A shrewd person, he understood the demand for increasing visibility, and managed to get regional rulers to provide substantial funds for organizing various colloquia.

Minister for Information Muhammad Abdul Ghaffar proposed holding an international conference in Manama in 2008 with the participation of the entire North Atlantic Council. He added that he was in favor of my idea to publish a newsletter on cooperation with the Alliance in Arabic.

Ghaffar went on to found the Bahrain Center for Strategic, International and Energy Studies, and we still see each other. He maintains that the street protests in Bahrain that began in February 2011 were instigated from abroad. He points his finger at Iran and its network of agitators. In his view, the lines between Sunni and Shiite communities in Bahrain are not as clear-cut as people would have you believe. Historically, there are no great basic differences, in his view, and the Shiites have no reason to choose armed rebellion.

Despite some criticism during the Obama years, the American administration has not condemned the Bahraini government for its repression as vigorously as some critics have hoped, limiting itself to blocking some loans. The King initiated a dialogue with the various factions and accepted a quite critical report by the United Nations that condemned the bloody repression of 2011. However, the situation is still evolving and we really have no idea of what the future holds in store.

In the United Arab Emirates, I had the impression that our overtures were carefully weighed, to understand how much the country would actually gain from them. (Until 1971 the Emirates went by the names of Pirate Coast and later the Trucial States.) With the UAE political leadership having given its green light, and since it was the army that had the greatest weight, my meetings were handled by the military authorities. They had substantial financial resources, and therefore could support ambitious initiatives, as the Chief of Staff confirmed to me directly.

In the end, the response was entirely positive. Indeed, the level of our relations progressively improved to the point that, in 2011, the UAE proposed opening an embassy to NATO in Brussels. Abu Dhabi was proud of the authority and status it had acquired in the preceding years.

As mentioned previously, the Crown Prince of Abu Dhabi, Mohammed bin Zayed Al-Molyan, was considered an innovator at an international level. He launched ambitious projects such as a local version of the Louvre.

However, I never would have imagined that one day the Emirates, using Italian air bases, would send their air force to contribute to bombardments against Qaddafi's regime in Libya. This was a clear political choice, confirmed by the UAE's presence at the NATO Summit in Chicago in May 2012. At times, you cannot believe your eyes!

Oman remains different. Peripheral to the major burning issues of the Middle East, it takes part in some Alliance activities and has opened an embassy in Brussels. However, it still has not formally adhered to the Istanbul Cooperation Initiative. On a number of occasions, I have met the Omani Minister of Foreign Affairs and high-level dignitaries. But, while impeccably courteous, they have not been prepared to take the next step with NATO.

It cannot be said that this will be enough to guarantee Oman's future or leave the road clear for its present leaders. There remains the fact that, in Muscat, the Al-Said dynasty has no direct heirs to the throne, and the Sultan, who has been in power since 1970, is reportedly not in good health.

You Go to Riyadh Only if
the King Signs Off on It

Saudi Arabia, not surprisingly, merits a separate chapter. Prince Turki bin Mohammed bin Saud Al Kabeer, whom I had met in Riyadh, visited Brussels several times, with full access to anyone he needed to talk with. Every time he left, he gave the impression of being satisfied, and that official adhesion to the Istanbul Cooperation Initiative would be more or less immediate. However, this never came about.

Each time it seemed that something was missing, but we never understood exactly what. Relations with the most important country of the Gulf were therefore left hanging in the air, and with each encounter we seemed to be starting again from the beginning.

Not wishing to repeat the experience of my first visit to Riyadh, I tried to make sure I had the right contacts. In this, I was able to use the good offices of Abdulaziz Sager, chairman and founder of the Gulf Research Center, headquartered in Jeddah. Dr. Sager is a man of culture, internationally known and respected, and we remain partners in some projects of our Foundations. He also has very good relations with the Saudi royal family. Being a prominent member of one of the families who are de facto custodians, on behalf of the King, of the sacred places in Medina only added to his prestige.

Finally, in mid-2006, an invitation arrived from Ambassador Saad bin Abdul Rehman Al-Ammar, Director General of the Saudi Foreign Ministry's Institute of Diplomatic Studies. He said that he intended to organize an official symposium on cooperation with NATO. The Minister for Foreign Affairs would be speaking, and there would be television and press to ensure official media coverage.

I was assured that King Abdullah had personally signed off on the decision. Therefore, there would be no further discussion. For once, the decision-making process had worked in my favor.

King Abdullah bin Abdulaziz Al Saud had ascended the throne upon the death of King Fahad bin Abdulaziz Al Saud in August 2005. On that occasion, as Acting Secretary General, I had sent a message of condolence. In reply, I received an elegant letter of thanks from the Saudi Chief of Protocol.

Already on my flight to Saudi Arabia, I got a sense of the country's complexity. I was seated next to a young woman, casually dressed, who mostly listened to music on her headphones, indistinguishable from her counterparts in Italy, Belgium, or the United States. When the pilot announced that we soon would be landing, she excused herself, returning ten minutes later, covered from head to toe in a black garment, with only her eyes showing, ready to disembark.

As for myself, I was met at the airport by some rather muscular gentlemen, who wore pistols over their white robes and were driving enormous Jeeps. A reception that made it quite clear no half-measures were taken when it came to ensuring the personal security of official guests.

I was invited to dinner at the King Faisal Center for Research and Islamic Studies, where I was cordially introduced to a number of leading personalities in both the political and intellectual fields. This is an important face of the Kingdom, where there is no lack of brain power with a deep knowledge of the world and with international reputations, including in the sciences. Still, this dinner was representative of the contradictions of the country. Of course, no alcohol was served, but what struck me more was the absence of women at the event, despite the fact that there are very accomplished women in Saudi Arabia, who certainly could have held their own with the men around the table

Along the road, I saw beautiful hotels with an attractive air, but I had to stay at the usual isolated government residence, under military guard. I entered an immense suite decorated with Louis XVI style furniture that must have made the fortune of some furniture maker.

The theme of the conference hosted by the Foreign Ministry was cooperation with the Atlantic Alliance. The entire Riyadh diplomatic corps had been invited, together with a series of civilian and military dignitaries, to provide an official seal for the conference. It was clear that things of this kind did not happen by chance. Behind it was the hand of a government that wanted the outside world to know that the subject was of serious interest to the country.

I had a long conversation with Minister of Foreign Affairs Prince Saud bin Faisal bin Abdulaziz Al Saud, as always, the consummate gentleman, who spoke with authority and knowledge. At this time, he was travelling less, and it was said that he had health problems, although he only passed away in 2015 in Los Angeles. The Minister was more positive than I had expected, repeating more than once that a partnership with NATO fit in well with the foreign policy of the country. He made it quite clear to me that the Ministry of Foreign Affairs was in favor of joining the Istanbul Cooperation Initiative.

He made it understood that he counted on formalizing this soon, and then went over regional issues that were of most importance to him. However, the official announcement of Saudi membership in the ICI never arrived. Rumors circulated that the anti-Western Chief of Staff was against the venture. This seemed to be confirmed by subsequent information, and presumably reflected the rivalry among factions, which Western observers have a hard time following in detail, though the general complexity of local politics is well known. So is, for that matter, the Al Saud dynasty's ability to navigate effectively in rough seas. For my part, I had my mantra about the potential added value for Saudi Arabia from a relationship with a capable group of developed countries like NATO.

There were even amusing episodes. For security reasons, my security detail did not want me to stay out in the open. They took me to an enormous shopping center where there were mostly women, veiled from head to toe. I jokingly asked the officers accompanying me how they managed to interact with women only through eye contact. They replied lightheartedly that they were used to it, and that in the end it was not so bad, because just with a glance they were able to understand a lot. It was with a certain degree of reluctance that I left this capital, so interesting, full of contrasts, and different from my usual haunts. Upon returning to Brussels, besides my official report, I recounted the details of the visit and my impressions to the American ambassador Victoria Nuland, given the particular US interest in Saudi Arabia.

The Arab Spring never reached the holy cities of the Kingdom with great force, although there were some protests even in Mecca and Medina. Beginning in 2011, responding to internal demands for change, the government reacted speedily with a substantial package of economic and social incentives. The figure of 170 billion dollars has been mentioned, and some long awaited political and social reforms were announced.

Riyadh, which feels it role as a regional power, also sent an army battalion to nearby Bahrain in 2011 to support the Sunni dynasty, in the face of protests by Bahrain's Shiite community. Significant loans have been issued to countries in fragile condition, starting with the more exposed ones, like Egypt and Jordan. For decades, in fact, Egypt has received strong support via Saudi loans, and in recent years the Kingdom has emerged as the real power confronting Teheran.

Opening up to New Players?

At a certain point, another problem arose: How to adapt our approach to changing international conditions? The partnership group we were addressing was made up of the Gulf countries and those included in the Mediterranean Dialogue. Did new interlocutors need to be added? The North Atlantic Council decided that the requisite political conditions to do this were a request by the country wishing to join and the agreement of all Alliance governments.

It seemed to me, at that time, that Yemen might be a natural candidate, as it was then formally associated with the Gulf Cooperation Council, although not yet officially a member. Yemen was still paying the price of Kuwait's coolness. The Kuwaitis remembered that there was not even a hint of protest from Sana'a about the 1990 invasion by Saddam Hussein.

As we are being reminded today, Yemen is a country of great strategic importance, in that it controls the mouth of the Red Sea and borders with Saudi Arabia and Oman. In Yemen, there is also a historic rift between Aden, a former British protectorate on the Indian Ocean, and the mountainous north.

I promoted the idea of opening to Yemen during a North Atlantic Council confidential discussion. I advanced the political and strategic reasons for engaging with Sana'a, including its geographical position. A serious debate took place on this question. The American ambassador was clearly in favor, while France raised objections. Others had no considered opinion on the matter.

In the end, I concluded that we should postpone the issue to another time, so that everyone would have a chance to reflect. However, the opportunity never presented itself, and Yemen remained left out. Whether this was positive or negative remains an open question. It was only in 2012 that Ali Abdullah Saleh, in power as a dictator for thirty-three years, was deposed and left the country. By then, Yemen was on the verge of becoming a failed state. Saleh was famous for having said that governing Yemen was "like dancing on the heads of snakes".

Lebanon is another country of enormous complexity that is well known, and about which there is no need for lengthy discussion. No one was inclined to get involved in its problems. Nevertheless, Beirut continued to be, and still is, an attraction for surrounding countries, while in other ways it was for years a political protectorate of Damascus. At present, Hezbollah holds the strongest cards in Lebanese internal politics.

When war broke out between Lebanon and Israel in 2006, Condoleezza Rice suggested interposing the Atlantic Alliance between the two sides. Proposals included a naval force to patrol the coasts to impede arms trafficking. In the end, nothing was done. However, in Washington, then Assistant Secretary of State for the Middle East David Welch told me that it had been useful to put forward an Alliance role, as this had put pressure on the United Nations to quickly find alternative solutions. Some countries, especially France, Welch argued, were extremely hostile to the idea of allowing NATO to enter the Middle East. This all led to a French-Italian agreement that summer to send in a UN-backed contingent to act as a cushion between the rickety Lebanese army, pro-Iranian Hezbollah, and Israel.

Already before the start of NATO's regional initiatives, the Palestinian Authority had represented an unsolved problem. It was embarrassing, since, in one way or another, the problem of how to deal with it always came up. The NATO Secretary General was convinced that it would be a good move for us to establish formal relations with the Ramallah authorities, but this would incite American opposition. Instructions from Washington left very little room for maneuver, despite the fact that almost all the other countries were in favor.

Still, it was clear that opening up to the Palestinians would earn us many points with Arab governments, and de Hoop Scheffer discreetly insisted on making this move. Finally, in 2005, there was a moment of apparent easing of tensions, and the director of the Secretary General's Private Office, Ed Kronenburg, visited Ramallah in June of that year, meeting with Palestinian leaders, including Saeb Erekat, the key man in negotiations with Israel. A return visit to Brussels was agreed upon, with the idea of creating some joint activities. High-profile ideas circulated in the Secretary General's Private Office, such as the possibility of training Palestinian security forces.

Then the Israel-Lebanon war broke out, and Israeli relations with the Palestinians inevitably worsened. Unfortunately, the initiative was shelved.

There were other moments in which the US accepted the principle of establishing projects for NATO cooperation with the Palestinians, as long as the political context was favorable. Unfortunately, in the end, some sort of crisis always seemed to break out, killing any prospects.

Whenever someone asked, the official line was that the Alliance was an inter-governmental organization and therefore opened partnerships with governments. It was not in a position to do so with an "authority," in other words, not an independent state. This was strictly speaking true, but was a clear political limitation.

Libya was for some time still off limits. True, the British had resumed diplomatic relations with Tripoli in 1999, after some progress in addressing the 1988 Lockerbie airliner bombing, which has been Libya's handiwork. The US reestablished relations with Libya in 2006, after the Libyans had been caught trafficking in nuclear technology and had moved to eliminate their weapons of mass destruction programs and stockpile. Still, a basic distrust of Qaddafi seemed to reign in Washington and London. Who knows, however, whether things ultimately would have gone differently in Libya if we had taken a different approach?

I had some personal experience of dealing with Libya from my time in the 1980s as head of the Italian Foreign Ministry office that dealt with European Economic Community (EEC) external relations. It seems that Abdessalam Jalloud, the number two in the Qaddafi regime, used to drop by for a drink at the Italian ambassador's residence in Tripoli. He launched the idea of moving closer to the EEC, of which Italy held the rotating presidency in the first six months of 1985.

Despite my skepticism, I was sent to Libya to get the specifics on this presumed opening, since I had responsibility for that region. At the airport, I found myself queuing up with Pakistani workers, until a soldier beckoned me into a room where I found a man waiting who spoke excellent Italian. "I am your counterpart," he said, accompanying me to the parking lot, where he ushered me into his car.

On the way to the hotel he explained that he had been the last minister of foreign affairs during the reign of King Idris, prior to Qaddafi's 1969 coup d'état, and that now he was given "ad hoc" assignments. On this somewhat shaky basis, I spent three days with him negotiating a text in which he said Italy should commit itself to make efforts on behalf of Libya, although he had no clear idea of exactly to what end. I soon understood that he didn't have the slightest idea what the EEC was. At a certain point, he mentioned that Libya was concerned about Spain's accession, but to my amazement admitted that they were not really sure about it, but they had read it in the Egyptian newspapers.

However, our roles reversed rapidly when he told me that he would be in serious trouble if my visit were considered unproductive. In fact, people were wandering around the hotel lobby and appeared to be checking whether we were really negotiating. These secret policemen managed to seem at the same time both threatening and ineffectual, and in some respects brought to my mind images from the Pink Panther movies. My stay included other bizarre episodes that I reflected upon in my room overlooking the seafront in Tripoli, while the television broadcast endless military parades.

Finally, I managed to draft a document that my interlocutor liked (and above all would please his superiors). It had that solemn tone he needed to prove his success to the government. But it was safely devoid of any commitment. I am happy to think that I helped him out and perhaps saved his job.

For All the Wrong Reasons, Syria is a Special Country

Damascus was considered off-limits. Washington viewed Syria as being joined at the hip with Iran and as a supporter of terrorism. Syria occupied Lebanon militarily until 2005 and was a patron of Hezbollah, along with Iran.

A friend of mine, a French archaeologist who had spent a long time in the country, told me that historically the Alawite minority had a very low social status. During the period of the French mandate, 1923–1946, the Alawites finally found an outlet in the armed forces, since the French Army of the Levant recruited from groups other than the Sunni majority, playing a game of divide and conquer. It was the military route that Hafez al-Assad, a career officer, used to come to power in 1970. He remained in power until his death in 2000, using a heavy hand whenever required. He was succeeded by his son, Bashar al-Assad.

Hafez became a leading figure in the Arab world during the 1960s and 1970s, earning the epithet "The Lion of Damascus." However, he also has gone down in history for the bloody repression of the 1982 uprising by the Muslim Brotherhood in Hama, resulting in thousands of deaths and the destruction of the city. This in turn earned him the inglorious name of "The Butcher of Hama."

An exponent of the Ba'ath Party, he came to power following a series of military coups d'état in the 1960s. At that time, the Ba'ath Party represented the "new face" of the Arab Renaissance. It is sad and perhaps also a bit unfair that this movement has passed into history because of Saddam Hussein and the al-Assad family.

Interestingly, in re-reading the pages written by a keen observer such as T. E. Lawrence, one finds passages already reflecting serious concern about Syria: "The verbal poverty of their Rome-borrowed name indicated a political disintegration. Between town and town, village and village, family and family, creed and creed, existed intimate jealousies sedulously fostered by the Turks" (*Seven Pillars of Wisdom*, Chapter 59).

I recently found my first published essay, which was on the Ba'ath Party and appeared in the Italian monthly *Relazioni Internazionali* (International relations) in 1968. While the Muslim Brotherhood in Egypt dates back to 1928, the Ba'ath Party was founded in April 1947 and was secular, transnational, and based on the ideology of a national Arab renaissance. Its founder was Michel Aflaq, a Syrian Christian. In the years that this book covers, the Americans had limited official relations with Damascus, and recalled their ambassador in 2005. The subsequent behavior of the al-Assad regime would seem to justify their caution.

I remember a meeting of NATO ambassadors in Brussels, where Steve Hadley, National Security Advisor to President Bush, who in 2005 had succeeded Condoleezza Rice, in no uncertain terms expressed the need for the political isolation of Syria. He was even a little sarcastic concerning European worries about maintaining a dialogue with Damascus. He pointed out that, while Washington was following a policy of excluding official visits, European governments were crowding the Syrian capital with their delegations. In any event, those cordial relations never brought about a change in the al-Assad regime's policies.

The Battle for Libya

The events discussed so far would form the background for NA-TO's decision to intervene in Libya in 2011. "The Battle for Libya" was the headline that Al Jazeera used every day for several months in that fateful year.

Regime change began in a most unexpected way. Truly, reality has a way of outrunning our imaginations, and the international community showed itself to be more disjointed than ever. The great rationalist Descartes would have been horrified if he had seen how the operation was conceived.

In the early days, the uprising spread like wildfire, despite Qaddafi's threats against those who dared to rebel. No one in the West understood very much about the situation on the ground in Libya, but everyone seemed to presume that it would end with the tyrant being expelled, like in Tunisia and Egypt.

However, it was soon evident that this expectation was erroneous. Qaddafi retained control of the armed forces, which set off to re-conquer Cyrenaica, the eastern part of the country, issuing threats of certain death to the rebels.

With the conquest of Benghazi only hours away, the West's cavalry arrived in the unexpected guise of "Marianne," France's national symbol. French President Nicolas Sarkozy, who had just finished flexing his muscle in sub-Saharan Africa by capturing the unfortunate president of the Ivory Coast, sent the French Air Force to Benghazi and saved the rebels.

An improvised coalition of various countries was formed, but French political hegemony did not go down well with the international community. In the end, NATO was charged with the task of carrying out air operations, applying the resolution approved by the UN Security Council literally as the people of Benghazi watched, with Qaddafi's tanks just a few meters away.

After the operation in Afghanistan, this was yet another poisoned apple for the Alliance. It can do everything, except what you need to do for a quick victory. To all intents and purposes, air superiority and bombardments are only useful if, at some point, those being bombed actually give up. However, it was politically unacceptable to conduct ground operations.

In the end, the rebellion was successful, but the methodology NATO employed to support it was not the best: a Tornado fighter-bomber here, a bomb there, some recognition here, the status quo there. All the while, the provisional government in Benghazi, which I had had the opportunity to meet, seemed to be decreasingly revolutionary and increasingly made up of gentlemen in double-breasted jackets. However, Mahmoud Jibril, the political leader during the hostilities, did show real leadership. He was a graduate of Cairo University and the University of Pittsburgh.

Compared to the usual scenarios, there were two novelties. The United States intervened in the unusual role of facilitator, without being on the front lines. They provided external support, but also seemed to treat NATO as a European organization, responsible for keeping order in its neighborhood. Washington was conveying the message that it did not consider North Africa to be of strategic importance. The de facto American slogan was "leading from behind".

The other novelty, less well covered by the media, was the fact that this intervention was only politically possible because of the Arab League's approval, something that in the past would have been inconceivable. The Gulf Cooperation Council conveyed the same message with its request for a no-fly zone over Libya.

Therefore, for the very first time, approval was given for a NATO military operation against an Arab country. The United Arab Emirates, Qatar, and Jordan even directly took part in the operations, with Morocco giving a hand. This too was something that had never been seen before.

This meant that everyone truly hated the Libyan dictator, or that *Realpolitik* can dictate previously unthinkable strategies. Surprisingly, the Saudi press was the first to call for the intervention of the Atlantic Alliance.

Obviously, the Gulf countries did not risk much in bombing Tripoli. Instead they gained merit points which could prove useful in the future, for example in the case of a threat from Iran.

Through all of this, and subsequently, the analysts would continue to understand very little about the Libyan tribes and their rivalries. Al Jazeera persisted in confused broadcasts directly from the Libyan sands, as if every day there were a battle underway. It was difficult to understand what was true.

To conclude, the truly new political element was not so much who governed in Tripoli, but rather that the new leaders had come to power thanks to NATO, with the express consent of the Arab League and the active contribution of some of its members.

In parallel, some cracks appeared in the Euro-Atlantic community. NATO's intervention was rather confused, as it was decided at the last moment, without the customary preparation to build internal political consensus. For the first time, only a minority of countries took part in the operations, with the clamorous abstention of Germany and Poland. From an operational point of view, the Alliance did well. It minimized collateral losses of civilians and damage to the country's infrastructure, but this positive aspect did not compensate for the loss of political unanimity.

A "Libya Contact Group," including diverse countries and international bodies, had basically given the political line to the North Atlantic Council, which historically had always proudly defended NATO's decision-making autonomy. This can be good or bad. We shall see the consequences of these innovations in the coming years.

We still do not know what political arrangement ultimately will bring stability to Libya. The most visible fact remains the infinite number of all types of weapons available. A very negative sign, since it implies a lack of confidence in the central government, which in truth does not have the necessary authority. A further problem lies in the absence of an international presence that is able to mediate effectively among the various factions.

I have seen similar cases: in Macedonia in 2001, when the country was on the verge of civil war, and then among the warlords in Afghanistan in 2003. In both cases, the presence of Alliance forces was successful in achieving demobilization.

After more than 40 years with Qaddafi in power, Libyan civil society was very underdeveloped. Who knows what balance of power will prevail in the end? To the surprise of many, the elections held in the summer of 2012 did not give the majority to extremist leaders, and Mahmoud Jibril, who so far appeared to be a moderate leader, achieved good results. Jibril, whom I know well personally, is a very intelligent and conceptual person. The contested 2014 parliamentary elections, on the other hand, did not help end the country's political divisions, and it is difficult to project the outcome of new elections planned for 2018. In the end, will the country remain unified?

It is perhaps ironic, even sad, that, after NATO and partners went to war to save the Libyan people, it subsequently has not been possible for the Alliance to forge a genuine partnership with Libya. Prime Minister Serraj, who heads the internationally-backed government in Tripoli, visited NATO Headquarters in June 2017 and secured a promise that NATO experts would assist in building defense and security institutions in Libya. Factional struggles, however, notably between Serraj and his main rival Khalifa Haftar, based in eastern Libya, remain a focus of concern for the NATO governments. One also has the sense that European governments are unsure of how to reconcile EU, NATO, and national approaches to dealing with Libya.

Let us wish the best to the Libyan people, who had to start again from zero to rebuild their country. But this is not a book about Libya.

Qatar: The Smallest Superpower in the World

My first visit to Qatar was in 2004. In Doha, I had met with Sheikh Hamad bin Jassim bin Jaber Al-Thani, who was then Minister of Foreign Affairs and became Prime Minister in 2007. He was also a highly successful entrepreneur, tall and with an energetic and lively appearance. He received me in a pavilion in the middle of a small garden. Wearing a traditional long white robe and using few words, he made it quite clear that he was strongly in favor of collaboration with the Alliance. He also suggested that I give an interview to Al Jazeera. I failed to follow up, however, as I felt it was premature at the time.

If there were any rivers in Qatar, we could say that a lot of water has flowed under the bridges since then. This almost uninhabited peninsula has been playing an unexpectedly prominent role, not just in economics and finance, but also in international politics, though in mid-2017 it also found itself in a difficult political crisis with Saudi Arabia and some other Arab states.

You could see the first signs of Qatar's new course in the visibility of Al Jazeera programs in both Arabic and English. However, few would have imagined that the former Emir Hamad bin Khalifa Al-Thani (who abdicated in 2013) would have pushed so far forward.

There is also no lack of questions and of conflicting analyses concerning his activism. And there was talk of a mysterious attack in Doha in September 2011, in which a number of bodyguards apparently died.

For many years, major Western countries simply viewed Qatar as an immense reserve of hydrocarbons, an inexhaustible source of energy with its 300 trillion cubic feet of natural gas, one of the largest reserves. I think this is exactly the image the country would like to avoid.

If we look at Qatar's history, it was dominated by the Persians, then the Ottomans, and finally the British. Since 1971 it has been in charge of its own destiny, and this is something it does not want to lose. It discovered only recently how its immense resources give it limitless freedom in a world dominated by the movement of large amounts of capital.

Consequently, the Emir wanted international recognition that was not dependent on oil and gas, but on the broader importance the country was acquiring in the world. Perhaps his first instinct was to make Qatar a destination and a point of reference for all sorts of interests. In this way, an enemy would not be able to suddenly overthrow the Al-Thani dynasty, because the rest of the world would object. The most likely candidates to destabilize the country would probably be Iran or a radical organization.

For this reason, foundations, universities, convention centers and institutions of every kind are constantly springing up in Doha. Even more surprising, it succeeded in being selected as the host for the 2022 Soccer World Cup, despite not having a soccer tradition. Of course, this is a difficult policy to follow, since it is not possible to adopt criteria for action that are totally transparent.

Qatar hosts the largest US military base in the Middle East, which has complicated relations between the Iranian ayatollahs and the Al-Thani dynasty. The Qataris at the same time have made important donations to questionable Palestinian organizations and armed movements. The Emir made an official visit to Gaza in October 2012. Despite this, Israel has a commercial office in the Emirate and the late Israeli president, Shimon Peres, made an official visit to Doha in 2007.

In light of Qatar's intrinsic vulnerability, these actions are geared toward acquiring a high profile in order to get protection from all sides. Qatar played an important role during the war in Libya, providing military advisors to the rebels and sending planes to take part in the bombing missions. This was an unprecedented historical event. There are also those who believe Qatar has an unscrupulous policy of sending aid to extremist Islamist movements in Libya, a choice that certainly could create problems for the Tripoli government.

Qatar has never held back, even with regard to Syria, and promoted an initiative to arm the rebels and to send a joint force from Arab countries. Before abdicating in 2013, Emir Hamad bin Khalifa Al-Thani, and his wife Sheikha Mozah, an international driving force in the creation of social and scientific research institutions, a complete novelty for the traditional societies of the region, had done a great deal to raise their country's profile.

I have the feeling that, from outside, it is difficult to understand the extent of Qatar's commitment to reconciling traditions and modernity. So far, Qatar has not witnessed any repercussions from the turmoil occurring elsewhere in the aftermath of the Arab Spring, which is something.

I personally got to know then Crown Prince Tamim bin Hamad Al-Thani, whom I first met on the eve of his wedding. He wore traditional white robes and was most cordial, ably putting his visitor at ease. He told me that he knew Belgium well, having spent a lot of time there. I mentally noted that nothing could be more different from Doha than the rainy Belgian forests. On another occasion, I could not resist the temptation of asking him more about his time there, and he explained to me that his family had property in Malmedy, a small German-speaking town. On my first visit, he was a young man, not yet in his thirties, who had studied in Great Britain and had been a cadet at Sandhurst. The Crown Prince roused my curiosity, since he represented a new generation of rulers who had had a good education and were open minded. Perhaps it will be up to them to decide the future? He is now Emir, following his father's unexpected abdication, he seems to me to be a good person and I wish him good luck.

Also contributing to my relationship with the country was my friendship with a young diplomatic couple in Brussels, Ambassador Meshal bin Hamad Al-Thani and his wife Alanood Al-Thani. He is currently Qatar's ambassador to the United States. They ably represented the ingenuity, optimism, and at the same time the tradition of their world, which is not just oil and skyscrapers. I remember Doha as a capital in the throes of rapid development, yet with a certain harmony, which overall made it attractive. Qatar is a country that is taking responsibility for the challenges of tomorrow.

I returned in September 2007, as my service to NATO was drawing to a close. As had occurred in Bahrain, Crown Prince Tamim Al-Thani warmly and politely thanked me for my efforts and for the good results attained. He expressed his satisfaction for the projects I was promoting with Qatar and other neighboring countries. He kindly praised me for my personal strong commitment to the cause of such an innovative project. After these expressions of respect, he asked me about my intentions for the future.

He maintained that the Arabian Gulf should become the main topic for joint examination, adding that the Alliance should become more seriously involved in the security of this area. In Doha, it was believed that the instability resulting from the civil war in Iraq and Iranian behavior would create a situation Qatar could not deal with on its own. They were also worried about the Afghan campaign, the recurrent episodes of intifada, and the war in Lebanon.

All good reasons for political consultations to take place alongside military ones. Seconded by Minister Al-Rumaihi, he proposed creating a training center in Doha under the banner and at the expense of Qatar, but with the guidance and expertise of the Atlantic Alliance.

I explained to them in all honesty that, to be successful, it was necessary to take things one step at a time. That was my friendly advice. First and foremost, it was necessary to strengthen the political will of NATO countries for any new commitments, otherwise it would be difficult to mobilize the resources necessary to carry out more ambitious projects.

I knew that, behind me at NATO, I had a collection of countries that would go forward as long as we took on narrowly defined commitments, commitments that brought prestige to everyone. However, there was not yet a deep-seated conviction in this regard. Even the United States had no clear line on the role of NATO relative to their bilateral relationships.

Then Chief of Staff General Hamad bin Ali Al-Attiya was a charming, hospitable and competent person. He is now Minister of Defense. With him it was possible to speak about training programs, consultations, intelligence, and so on. He would have liked to contribute to the effort in Afghanistan, but Qatar's somewhat limited national armed forces were already committed in Lebanon under the aegis of the United Nations.

Having found out it was my birthday, besides the customary medal, he gave me a watch, which one of his assistants handed me at the airport right before leaving. It is a pocket watch, which I have kept as a welcome reminder of the General and our work together.

Already in those days, the emirate attracted visits from leading world figures, and on that occasion I happened to brush past Cherie Blair, wife of the British Prime Minister, at the Ritz-Carlton Hotel, while she was being courted by various dignitaries, who were circling around her. Just for the record, the hospitality of the Qatar government was always splendid, and on that occasion I was provided with the most elegant suite I had ever seen in my life. We ended up taking a dip in the Ritz-Carlton swimming pool, magnificently located below the artificial waterfall of that incredibly lavish and sumptuous hotel.

What I also remember of that moment was my plea to my closest collaborators. I asked that, after I left, they continue wholeheartedly the work with the Arabs that had begun so well.

Lines in the Sand

Especially for Europe, the West's relations with the Arabs go back to ancient times. Sometimes we have difficulty remembering this, above all if it implies some kind of responsibility. Protectorates, mandates, etc. The old Suez Canal Company and the oil concessions granted to European and American companies were textbook examples. In some countries "capitulations" were in force, which meant Europeans had the right not to be judged in local courts, but by special courts controlled by their respective countries. Political or economic development was only of interest for its consequences for London, Paris or Berlin, who were competing among themselves for influence over the region.

This is not ancient history. Syria, Lebanon, Jordan, Iraq, and Palestine were divided up between France and Great Britain in 1921-23. The background is described in detail in *A Line in the Sand: Britain, France and the Struggle That Shaped the Middle East* (2011), an excellent book by the English journalist James Barr, who describes something reminiscent of Rudyard Kipling's "Great Game," the competition between the great powers in Central Asia at the end of the 19th century.

The Arab peoples were pawns in the game between the colonial powers. A reversal in this tendency really only occurred in 1956, when US President Eisenhower intervened to end the Anglo-French military operation to take control of the Suez Canal. But it is also true that, during the Cold War, both blocs had their own clients in the Middle East, and sought to use their clients against each other.

The Key External Actors

Looking at the current situation, the Europeans are the ones who have the most to gain from political stability and social development in countries that are so nearby, especially in North Africa and the Levant. But the Arab Spring took the corridors of power in Brussels by surprise, and the panorama of the European Union (EU)'s "neighborhood policy" has not been thrilling. Despite the fact that, for almost 40 years, we have been talking about "Mediterranean policy."

In reality, this has never been a high priority, because Eastern Europe always came first, thanks to excellent advocates like Germany and Poland, as well as the possibility for accession to the EU. Also, we know from experience that EU mechanisms are complex, and that it takes a long time to get results. Perhaps too, the EU's External Action Service is still only in its early days, and we will have to wait until they acquire more experience.

We certainly cannot be decisive but, even so, we can have a positive influence as the Arabs follow the difficult road they have before them. Our civil society can play a role, just as governments can. It is also true that Arab countries sometimes engage in behaviors that are inconsistent with EU rules. I remember that, in the 1990s, Egypt was eligible for a quota of 30,000 tons of rice for export to the European Union market. Then Egypt asked for 100,000 tons to renew the agreement, even though it did not produce enough rice to meet that quota. But the result was that the European producers got scared and the agreement was delayed for many years. The Egyptian negotiators admitted in private that they knew this, but wanted to take a hard line for public consumption at home.

In any case, in the political field Washington is the primary player and pays special attention to the Arabian Peninsula, where the US has major interests and which it considers a priority on the world scale. There has been a large US presence in the area since the 1940s. In turn, the US has little strategic interest in North Africa, as was shown in 2011 by the limited support the US provided in Libya.

The US is without a doubt the country that in recent decades has invested the most in the Middle East in political, economic and military terms. For two or three generations, America has played a prominent role in the Arab world via universities, foundations, and civilian and military assistance. It gives Egypt two billion dollars a year, most of which goes to the armed forces. Only Israel receives more assistance than Egypt.

This doesn't mean that America is popular in the region. The 2003 invasion of Iraq turned out to be a real disaster, which continues to take its toll. The result before our eyes is a fragile and poorly governed Iraq, where ISIS is just barely kept at bay, thanks in part to direct intervention by Iran. Even the re-conquest of Mosul in summer 2017, by Iraqi forces, with US and Kurdish support, seemed unlikely to solve the ISIS problem once and for all. We have to acknowledge, however, that the Obama administration inherited a difficult situation, and perhaps because of this US policy was more cautious than in the past.

However, looking closely, Washington's influence is still very strong in the Gulf and the Arabian Peninsula. It is also the part of the Arab world where the "awakening" that rocked other countries has had fewer repercussions.

The overall situation in the region, however, is confused, and the underlying Sunni-Shi'a conflict has become a distinctive feature in the context of the political disarray. At the moment, neither the international community broadly speaking, nor the Arab League specifically, have any influence on the situation. The only step towards conciliation was the agreement with Iran on nuclear materials production, to which the United States and the rest of the international community devoted enormous effort for many years.

Henry Kissinger maintains that American foreign policy, unlike any other country's, is based on ethical principles and ideals. In *Diplomacy*, he writes that otherwise it would not be possible to understand the United States, which historically has considered itself the land of freedom and democracy. Kissinger concludes that no country has been more pragmatic in the conduct of its foreign policy, but also more ideological in following its convictions.

In effect, in 2011, the year of the Arab Spring, the Obama administration generally took the side of the popular and reformist movements. Once the electoral process had started in Egypt, in Washington it seemed inevitable that they would have to accept the consequences. This was a bet that did not pay off. Despite years of US investment in the Egyptian armed forces, Mohammad Morsi's victory meant that the US found itself dealing with the Muslim Brotherhood, a very different group, with no experience in governing. The fact that the US dumped Mubarak so abruptly made leaders in other friendly countries worry that they would meet the same fate.

The Muslim Brotherhood then clumsily tried to concentrate power in its hands. This was confirmation that parliamentary democracy was not just a matter of elections, but that, to succeed, democratic traditions had to be consolidated over time, in a favorable social climate. What happened next is well known. The pendulum swung in the opposite direction, leading to the military regime of Abd El-Fattah El-Sisi. The Americans and Europeans both would love to see the leaders in Cairo have more conciliatory internal policies, but have to deal with reality.

We should not forget that, in the 1950s, there was a first Arab awakening under the banner of nationalism. Then as well, relations between Washington and Cairo went sour. After Nasser took power in 1952, an American delegation secretly went to Cairo to meet him. The meeting took place in a secret location, where it is said Nasser put two packs of Kent cigarettes on the table and began to smoke one cigarette after another.

The American emissaries began by saying they were prepared to provide substantial economic and military assistance, on the condition, however, that the aid would be delivered via a permanent military mission in Cairo. Nasser reacted angrily, saying that, after having succeeded with great effort in throwing the English out of the country, he had no intention of bringing in new "protectors." Egypt went its own way and a historic opportunity was lost.

Turkey is another actor that has moved into the spotlight in the 21st century. The Erdogan government does not hide its grand political ambitions, and has rediscovered the Arab region as a natural zone of influence. Not surprising, since the Ottoman Empire was the dominant power there until 1918. This is probably what caused Turkey's break with Israel, interrupting a long period of friendship. One has the impression, however, that the Ankara government overestimated its influence with the Arabs and that this policy is not obtaining the desired results. For example, Turkey supported the Muslim Brotherhood in Egypt and now is bitterly critical of the military regime.

Russia has a historic Mediterranean policy that dates to time of the czars. It also has important interests in certain specific countries. Qaddafi's disappearance went down badly with Moscow, but it maintains its special relationship with the Damascus government. Therefore, it could play a significant role in finding an internationally acceptable solution to the Syrian conflict.

China and India are new actors in the greater Arab region. Because of their growing economic interests, they are much more involved than in the past, but their long-term role is not yet clear.

As for Italy, it is a natural interlocutor. It is important, but has no hegemonic ambitions. It can have an important role in policy towards the Mediterranean and the Middle East both on its own and in Brussels. Italy has an active and widespread civil society with which to make contacts in the realms of culture, sports, communications, and education. There is still a tendency to think of governments as the exclusive actors in the international arena, but, if you look closely, they actually have a limited capacity to influence many key factors of change.

Speaking of external actors, you can't avoid looking at the West as a whole, which is not without its own problems. We often see parliamentary democracy in difficulty. Populism is gaining strength, and, in the view of many critics, business has excessive influence on governments. Mass communications and social media have become crucial, but emotions are in the forefront, with manipulation often right around the corner. Analysis becomes of secondary importance, and the drama of events prevails in decision-making

As always, we know where we have been, but not where we are going. Honestly, we do not have a clear idea how democracy, an incredible achievement for which we have fought bitterly, will evolve. There is a well-known quip by Winston Churchill: "It has been said that democracy is the worst form of Government, except for all those other forms that have been tried from time to time." In Western democracies, the desire to assume responsibility and to count for something in the world is diminishing. A development that would be in some ways understandable, if it signified respect for the values of others and acceptance of new actors.

The creation of new international forums like the G-20 is certainly more representative of reality. However, the multilateral method is still a novelty for the large emerging nations. Europe and North America, on the other hand have been accustomed for many decades to this kind of negotiations, where it is understood that everyone has to give up something.

Said in another way, representativity has improved while world governance is visibly marking time. The international community is not very cohesive, even though issues affecting the planet are ever more connected. Proof of this are the European Union's own problems in making progress on an immigration policy.

The European Union is an extraordinary project that put an end to centuries of bloody wars and violent conflicts. Today, however, it seems to be having an identity crisis, and is suffering in its search for new, shared objectives. Perhaps enlargement occurred too fast, not allowing the time needed for in-depth study. Public opinion is confused. On one hand, there are protests because Brussels wants to regulate too much. On the other, they complain because the EU is not able to do enough on important issues and toward the rest of he world.

Despite the complexity of the challenges, if we look at security issues, the international community has not created new mechanisms, and those that exist are not in good shape. European defense policy appears weak, and has not taken off, in spite of expectations. For their part, the Americans are more oriented toward alliances formed from time to time for specific objectives. In a certain sense it is easier, but "coalitions of the willing" do not create solid shared values or common interests and do not improve the functioning of the international community.

The Atlantic Alliance, which for a long time has represented Western democracies well, remains an effective operational vehicle. In 2014, it concluded with dignity its mission running the UN-mandated International Security Assistance Force in Afghanistan. But its prestige has been diminished, its member governments are less cohesive, and the Euro-American relationship is not what it used to be, also because there are other priorities in the world.

When the Men with the Beards Arrive

In the complex and confusing context just described, the events usually referred to as the Arab Spring caught everyone by surprise. However, it had been known for a long time that there was a problem of political immobility in many countries. A quick examination shows that, in Egypt, Libya, Tunisia, Algeria, Saudi Arabia, and Yemen, heads of state had been in power for 30 or 40 years. We have seen that succession is easier in the monarchies, where there is usually an heir to the throne. They have held up better because they have more legitimacy.

In the authoritarian republics, which lack any established procedures for the transfer of power, autocrats tend to propose their sons as successors. In Egypt in 2010, thoughts regarding Mubarak's successor focused on whether or not the military leadership would accept his son Gamal. Syria, where the al-Assads have perpetuated Alawite rule since 1970, also is a textbook case. In Libya, they were considering Qaddafi's sons.

The hopes stimulated by the many movements, supported by large numbers of young people in the region, gradually have given way to disappointment, restoration, and sometimes chaos. Tunisia is the only country that seems to be moving towards democratic norms, but even there with many difficulties.

The Islamic State's unexpected successes, and its barbaric practices that seem to come from long-forgotten eras, are creating anxiety everywhere. Iraq's persistent internal fragility and vulnerability, the interminable Syrian civil war, and the bloody crisis in Yemen are violent scenarios that we have no idea how to deal with.

A few truths that we did not understand well have emerged from underneath the ashes. The first is that few countries had a real historically solid structure, perhaps only Morocco, Tunisia, and Egypt. This is a tremendous handicap. Other countries, like Jordan, Iraq, and Syria are states that were created for foreign political reasons.

The second is the weakness of civil society, despite the progress underway. Lastly, there is the excessive role of religion in the civil sector and the lack of a historic foundation for democracy. When there are elections, the natural tendency of the winner is to seize all the power, as we saw in Egypt with the Muslim Brotherhood. The principle of power sharing still seems to be unknown.

Movements of Islamic inspiration for the moment are in the majority, because they hark back to a common cultural reference point. We don't know what kind of relationship to cultivate with these bearded men, even when their movements, like the Muslim Brotherhood, are not extremist. Our culture tells us that we should have a dialogue with them, but in the current political phase it is a very difficult task.

Another worrisome factor is that the Arab League's façade of solidarity disappeared some years ago. The countries of the League today move in different ways. There is not just the Sunni-Shi'a dividing line, but we see divergent perceptions among the Sunnis themselves, for example Turkey towards Egypt or the Gulf states toward Qatar.

These are all nasty surprises, even if many of us believed that there inevitably would be turbulent years in the transition from the old political systems to other more representative ones, though without the extremes we are seeing today. Remember that, even in Europe, almost a century passed after the revolutions of 1848 before democratic norms were consolidated. In this situation, it is probably better to avoid making political predictions, because there are just too many variables.

Some countries have managed to remain out of the fray. For example, the King of Morocco knew how to preempt any incidents by supporting a moderate coalition government and some reforms. In time, we will see whether his strategy truly has worked.

It is interesting that Algeria was not involved in the revolts. Perhaps this was due to the very recent memory of their bloody internal war with radical Islamism. There is also the fact that Algeria is a country with a secular tradition and a large female presence in parliament and the universities.

Iran should not be confused with the Arabs, but it is only a step way from the region and has significant weight in Iraq, Syria, Lebanon, and Gaza. The nuclear accord concluded with the international community in 2015 brought a sigh of relief, and has been the only positive thing that has emerged from that geographic horizon. Naturally, questions about the evolution of the country's clerical regime still remain.

In this world of major challenges, the Israelis are following developments and holding their breath, trying not to be dragged into the fray. However, their relations with the Palestinians are more unresolved than ever, a permanent frustration that slowly is distancing the country from the approval of the international community.

A Look Beyond the Horizon

It is difficult to end these reflections without trying to understand the deep motives behind the situation in the Arab world, even if the bookshelves are starting to creak under the weight of books about the Arabs. The situation is so complex, and the flux of events so rapid, that one is tempted give up on writing analyses. But the story does not end here. On the contrary, it seems that we are only at the beginning of a process, and do not know where it will lead.

As I write, many things are changing in unpredictable ways. Taken in perspective, perhaps the Arab region, somewhat painfully, is aligning itself with historical trends elsewhere in the world. Other parts of the world in fact have completed journeys to better political and social systems. You only have to think about Latin America, where in the 1980s almost every president was in a military uniform, and today there is not one military government. In 1989, the Soviet Union and Eastern Europe system had been immobile for two generations. Then suddenly, it was gone. In recent decades we have seen an increase in economic wealth, relationships between countries, communications, and even more participatory forms of government.

For a long time, the Middle East and North Africa seemed insulated from change, in the grip of unacceptable regimes and immobile societies, dogged by corruption and the other problems of rentier states. Despite the difficult road they have before them, hundreds of millions of people keep alive their hope of taking their destiny into their own hands.

And the economy?

This book is not about economics and finance, but it is clear that economic development is a fundamental factor. First, you must take into consideration that, in the Middle East and North Africa, there is no form of regional integration. The actors are fragmented, which does not help the countries face development problems or deal cooperatively with challenges.

Secondly, exportation of non-petroleum products has been stagnant for a long time, while other geographical areas have increased their quota of international trade. In other words, it is a region that is not growing, and that has not profited from globalization. In the past 20 years, growth in per capita income in the Middle East has been around 0.5 percent, lower than in the other regions of the world. Latin America and Africa have more than double that rate, without speaking of Asia. As for youth unemployment, the rate consistently has been above 30 percent.

The clear implication is that, in order to pursue development that is in line with the rest of the world, the rules must be changed to make more efficient use of existing resources. Naturally, this process is anything but easy, and over time will require profound readjustments and a favorable climate, which in general is not present today.

From the point of view of capital, the rich countries of the Gulf obviously have an important role. In recent years, Saudi Arabia has injected robust doses of capital into its own economy to satisfy internal expectations, as well as furnishing financial assistance essential for the stability of Egypt and Jordan. Qatar has done the same things, but these were emergency responses that did not resolve structural problems.

The financial system of the Gulf countries is rather well developed and has a transnational dimension that, quite understandably, looks toward India, the rest of South Asia, and China. However, not even Saudi Arabia has infinite resources, and the big drop in the price of oil in the medium term can have negative implications. There has also been talk of Jordan and Morocco joining the Gulf Cooperation Council to safeguard the two monarchies.

Political disorder and uncertainty are very harmful. In Egypt, we saw a drop in tourism and investment, the negative side of social protest. In Tunisia, the same effect occurred because of terrorist attacks that had international resonance. Libya is in chaos. The oil industry infrastructure, practically the country's only source of wealth, is at risk. At risk is even the basic ability of people to live together. Since 2011, illegal emigration has been one of the most painful aspects of this situation that has spun out of control. Iraq too has been unable to recover normality since 2003, and needs profound economic reforms that are highly unlikely in the current situation.

One positive piece of news on the energy front concerns the enormous gas deposits that have been found in the eastern Mediterranean, between Israel, Lebanon, and Cyprus. Exploitation of this resource will provide energy independence for this area, and also help Jordan. Europe could take advantage of these new resources as well and diversify its energy sources.

Conclusions

At this point, the questions are: Was the effort involved in NATO's strategic rapprochement with the Arabs in the political-military field worth it? What were the results? Was it a success? Can we learn from these experiences?

The response to all these questions is decidedly positive. The Atlantic Alliance did well to go in this direction and to give it a purely practical and not legalistic content. These were good initiatives in an environment that was anything but receptive. It is clear that we can't call this a success with a capital "S". However, in these pages we have seen how relations gradually grew from the end of 2003 to 2007-2008. In those years, substantial progress was made.

The question then follows: Will this approach continue, and in what way? Here the answer is somewhat more doubtful, because we do not know how political priorities will develop. Will NATO continue to be relevant and maintain the vision that is described in this book? And at what speed, given that today the traditional Euro-Atlantic community is less cohesive.

The hope is that the connections established so far will grow and strengthen in the long run, but it is clear that things do not happen by themselves, if there is no political incentive. There is also the risk that one country will block the partnership's activities for its own reasons.

We are witnessing a major return to bilateralism, which in fact implies less solidarity with others and an "every man for himself" spirit, despite the fact that the planet's problems are ever more complex and interaction among peoples continues to increase.

There is a need for better "governance" in an ever-widening world where the leadership of the West no longer exists, where there are new, inexperienced actors emerging, and where there are different forms of government and societies that reflect different values. The approach described in these pages anticipated new roads for the future of international relations. It merits attention and recognition because it tried not to impose anything, but rather, offered concrete "added value" with no strings attached, moving in the direction of shared responsibility, where the key words were "knowledge," the "search for agreement," and "deciding together".

We tried to expand the experience acquired by Europe and North America over the course of a half-century in the field of security, where NATO's authority was recognized by all. The proof is in the facts, including the participation of various Arab countries in actions to bring down the Libyan regime, which at the time seemed strong. In practice, we created new relationships among people who had never met each other, and a more shared vision based on multilateral cooperation and the search for common interests. There are growing numbers of Arabs who are studying strategic problems alongside Europeans and Americans. This can only be viewed as a positive, since our culture gives particular importance to democratic control of the military, transparency, and public opinion.

At the same time, we have to admit that events risked thwarting this approach at every step. Unresolved issues, nuclear threats, local wars, and diverging perceptions were not lacking. There were always problems to resolve. Large international organizations have many voices and are difficult to manage. Within them, you can only keep moving by exerting constant pressure on their components. We also must recognize that, out of habit, many members retain a parochial outlook and have little familiarity with the wider world.

Creating a common culture is a long and difficult exercise.

Therefore, consolidating these results will continue to require active work for many years. In the Arab world, you are generally dealing with highly intelligent people, albeit conditioned by the complexities of their societies, something all of us admittedly can experience to some degree. You should not forget the frustrations that derive from history, including the tendency to think that Westerners try to obtain advantages for themselves and give nothing in return. But, when you are recognized as trustworthy and as a bearer of useful things, the relationship can change, and closed doors can open.

In the final analysis, this book is a narrative about decisions that were taken in a moment of great historic change, and how we tried to apply them in creating an architecture to bring North Africa and the Middle East closer to the West. Someone might turn up his nose and suggest that the Atlantic Alliance was in fact the actor in this process. It is worthwhile then to repeat that NATO is the leading organization in the political-military and strategic field. It is the best mix of experience, culture, and respect that exists.

The risk in writing a story with so many events and such undeniable complexity is that it will seem too dry. However, behind the facts, there are always people with their emotions, uncertainties, desires, and fears. There were moments of excitement when we thought we were able to achieve what we wanted, and moments of disappointment when things seemed to be going badly. In the events described in this book, I would say that, for everyone involved, the human aspect always counted a great deal.

In taking on this mission, I was determined to take advantage of that window of opportunity and to succeed. I created a task force in the International Staff to ensure that policy decisions were concrete and permanent. This was of great help, but it is undeniable that there were sectors where we made little progress. For example, in my time we were not very successful in launching scientific programs, whereas NATO had been able to organize projects even with the Soviet Union.

I did the things described in these pages with conviction and, I must add, received unexpected personal satisfaction, like the warm wishes of the current Emir of Qatar and the Crown Prince of Bahrain on my farewell visits. They thanked me for opening doors that had previously been closed, for the will to move the process forward concretely, and for the architecture that I had designed with them. And, of course, there was the support of the North Atlantic Council for these efforts, plus its recognition of the progress made.

The participation of Arab partner countries in NATO's Operation Unified Protector in Libya in 2011 was not an end point, but rather a milestone along a continuing path toward intensified cooperation. A number of Mediterranean Dialogue countries (Egypt, Jordan, Morocco, and Tunisia) plus all the members of the Istanbul Cooperation Initiative take part in the Global Coalition against ISIS/Daesh, an effort NATO strongly supports. In January 2017, the NATO regional training center in Kuwait opened, with the participation of the North Atlantic Council. The NATO Defense College Foundation, which I founded a number of years ago, has encountered nothing but intense interest during its outreach to the Middle East, and even the Arab League reportedly has been reaching out to authorities in Brussels, to discuss technical assistance.

This continuing evolution encourages me to think that the Alliance's approach, going back to the aftermath of the Iraq crisis, was the right one. I believe we were able to offer a concrete, transparent, and coherent approach at a very difficult time, without creating unreasonable expectations. I also believe there is room for continued growth, though this of course will require leadership on all sides that preserves the will to build solid cooperation on defense and security, support reform processes, promote best practices, and strengthen civil-military relations. An international organization is a complex body, which can achieve a little or a lot. All depends on the political will of its member governments

Indeed, there is one last broad lesson we can learn from this. Western societies, that is to say our democracies, cannot only be spectators of the very complicated world of the Greater Middle East. There is a wide range of possibilities for action in reasonable and concrete dimensions.

There is a wealth of humanity that deserves our best wishes and is not easy to forget: the people who live among the ancient mosques in Cairo, the Roman cities of Jordan, the pearl islands of the Arabian Gulf, and the deserts of Mauritania. They are the bearers of so much history and humanity, and they deserve a better future! We face a great world in flux, which requires us to take a long view, out toward a new horizon in our history. And finally, we should remember that many people, of different callings, are traveling the roads of this complex world, with the desire to understand and to help. We should always spare a thought for them.

Epilogue: The Concert of Nations in a Changing World.
Where is Multilateralism Going?

It is interesting to observe how intergovernmental relations, and particularly international organizations, actually function on a day-to-day basis, as opposed to how they are portrayed in textbooks. Indeed, it is difficult to understand how events such as those described in this book develop, unless you have at least a rough idea of how governments and multilateral diplomacy work in reality. I hope that these notes will help in understanding this process. Looking at things from the outside, you could get the incorrect impression that important international events unfold in an almost mechanical way.

Operating in a multilateral context is generally considered an area for specialists, in contrast to traditional bilateral diplomacy. As diplomatic professionals in a bilateral setting, we know how to work for our own governments in relation to another government, or at least we think we do. In other words, we act in line with our own national authorities, give importance to certain activities, follow matters in the way we have been taught, and so on.

In a multilateral setting, the work is less clear. There are special procedures for decision-making: unanimity, consensus, qualified majority. How to achieve the desired outcome? In multilateral diplomacy, it is necessary to "keep everyone together" by seeking compromises on difficult choices, focusing on the final objective, and envisioning a path to get there. It is immediately apparent that this is quite a different game. Working in multilateral diplomacy is also very interesting, because you acquire knowledge about other countries, how they function, how decisions are made, their guiding principles, as well as their basic policies.

It is also highly useful. Sometimes, however, you have some-what bizarre experiences, such as when I received an invitation to dinner from the head of a major European intelligence service. I arrived in the country's capital after having carefully studied the political issues that I believed were of interest to them. I was expecting a consultation on strategic issues. Instead, I discovered at the end of the dinner in a beautiful isolated villa that they were really interested in being invited to certain special meetings in Brussels in place of another "rival" service from the same country. They thought that I would have influence on this kind of decision.

In a political organization, the most important governments admittedly end up being the majority shareholders, because they know how to leverage their weight to use the multilateral instrument with greater skill to achieve their foreign policy objectives. It is said that, in international politics, it is not possible to quantify objectives, therefore it is not possible to evaluate the efficacy of actions. This is only partially true, as achieving results relative to objectives can be measured in foreign policy.

In the multilateral context, certain types of players acquire weight: those who propose concrete initiatives, who want to achieve results, who place great importance on their image as winners, and who make decisions with relative ease. They are essential to the system, since they are to all intents and purposes the main driving force.

A classic example is the United States, an indispensable player without which the multilateral machine would move with great difficulty. They have on their side both strength and the ability to make choices, and therefore wield enormous influence.

On strategic problems, i.e. issues that cross over political and military lines, London and Paris are still influential. France has a significant interdiction power that it often implements in an unscrupulous way to increase its visibility or extract concessions. Germany, although a country of great prominence, has to contend with a growing pacifist component.

Given that consensus is a prerequisite, the dynamics of negotiations among members of an organization naturally also highlight the governments that are willing to block decisions. When one country prevents achievement of an overall consensus, something that happens more frequently than one might imagine, the organization's efforts usually focus on the recalcitrant delegation, and other members may make concessions that otherwise would not have been considered.

In everyday practice, there is a natural tendency for countries to follow the majority that forms on the issues under discussion. There are also special cases, however, such as Greece and Turkey, which become highly sensitive when discussing issues that touch on their national interests. I remember, for example, long and fruitless negotiations with the ambassadors of Greece and Turkey, both personal friends, to verify, down to the very last comma, the meaning of international conventions governing navigation. For years, Greece has been blocking Macedonia's accession to NATO solely because it refuses to recognize the country's name, fearing that one day it will lay claim to Greek Macedonia.

It is always necessary to have an idea where you want to arrive in negotiations, as well as knowing the details of the technical issues, to be able to react quickly to the contents of a document. It obviously implies the will of diplomats to fully support national positions, and to know how to advance them throughout the process. Not everyone has this skill. These features give an advantage to governments that have clear lines of action, analytical skills, and are ready to negotiate the details. In other words, those having a strong bureaucracy and robust policy directives.

Because of its basic character, this system gives greater visibility to countries that do more operationally. This is not openly declared as a basic principle, however, as some suppose. Among the Europeans, France and the UK have the ability to put together an above average political-military instrument. This is not surprising, as both in Paris and in London there are historic traditions of influencing others, and no difficulty in taking positions on the problems of the day. As seen in many parts of the world, what the British were best at was being colonial governors. I discovered at NATO that Turkish diplomats also have excellent traditions and represent their important country effectively, while taking a broad overall view.

Italy also has a good diplomatic tradition. Its problem is not the quality of the diplomats, but identifying specific objectives it can sustain over the long term. Although Italy does not normally figure among the three or four crucial world protagonists, it plays a significant role in providing real contributions when decisions have been taken. We can say that, thanks to its concrete contributions, Italy historically has been a member of the Atlantic Alliance's leadership group. It was able to develop recognized capabilities, including the Carabinieri military police, who have made important contributions in many places, beginning in Bosnia, where Italy was the first country to provide badly-needed gendarmerie-type forces.

How you present your arguments is the first condition for success in multilateral initiatives. One must not be too generic or too informal, but rather demonstrate in-depth technical knowledge of the issue being discussed. In your presentation, you must highlight what may be of interest to your interlocutor, try to understand their country's point of view, and if possible their personal point of view.

A question that arises constantly, and with which I have had to deal many times, is how to effectively leave a clear message with an otherwise distant and unknown counterpart, when you have only one opportunity to convince them, for instance in a 45-minute meeting. This is no easy exercise. It involves a mixture of authority, simplicity, and ability to attract attention, while leaving the impression that the discussion will continue in the future. This is essential training to obtain results that can last over time.

In the field of traditional bilateral diplomacy, i.e. between two governments, the logic and methodology are obviously different. First of all, the objectives can be shared more easily, the hierarchical line is more precise, and people's careers are influenced by well-identified lines of authority.

If we look at international organization officials, their objectives may vary, and their loyalty to the institution they work for is not always certain. Sometimes they are temporarily provided by a member state, receiving a salary from their capital and not really willing to follow the directives of others. In truth, nationality always remains an important factor in international organizations, although in theory it should not be so.

I have realized with time and experience–at NATO, the European Union and in other contexts–how important it is to monitor closely how decisions taken at the political level are applied in practice; tasks and objectives must be clearly indicated to those responsible for carrying them out. Of course, there are also positive aspects: dealing with people from various countries, there is a greater professional and cultural breadth, and it is possible to tap into a wide variety of different cultures and skills.

Working in such environments, you can have some special opportunities. In 2006, for example, I met with the Archbishop of Smolensk, who is now Patriarch of the Russian Orthodox Church under the name Cyril I. He came to Brussels accompanied by several priests from other denominations. His purpose was to emphasize the need to respect Russian specificities and traditions in the political dialogue with Moscow. He felt so strongly about these issues that the meeting went on for over two hours. I was not prepared for this, but did my best to reassure him that, in contemporary European culture, diversity is an essential component. Using Italy as an example, I explained that, in one Italian province, German is the first language. I cannot say to what extent I was successful, but I hope that I was able to leave him with a reasonably good impression.

The slogan "effective multilateralism" has been coined to indicate that we must ensure that the system does not remain inert and is able to take real decisions. We know that the effectiveness of international organizations is measured by their ability to make decisions. These criteria are the object of heated debate, because they make all the difference between unilateralism and multilateralism.

Europeans are traditionally more loyal to the broad multilateral approach, often criticized for its slowness in the United States, where the "coalition of the willing" has been in fashion. With these coalitions, the United States can undertake military operations together with countries that are with them from time to time, in order to achieve a specific goal. This allows for quick action, since there are no procedures, committees, deadlines, common rules, or discussions, which are the essence of the multilateral system.

An international organization is certainly slower, but it has far greater political legitimacy, and ensures that decisions are better thought through. The NATO campaign that led to Kosovo's self-determination in 1999 was a textbook case. According to the prevailing view in Europe, it was a positive example. In America, however, there was talk of unnecessary delays as a result of a military operation being led "by committee."

Many believe that the big decisions are taken by legions of experts, based on carefully considered data and assessments. In most cases, however, it is not so. What counts much more are the personalities of the protagonists or the political assessment of the moment. This is hard to admit since, to a certain extent, we still tend to mythologize history.

In fact, if we look at the behavior of governments from a concrete historical perspective, we can often see improvisation or blatant errors of judgment, often dramatic ones, such as those that led to the outbreak of World War I, which caused endless suffering, and which prepared the ground for the disasters caused by Nazism, World War II, and the Holocaust. We know that all this came about almost by accident, because some sovereigns, ministers, and generals of the great powers did not understand one another, attributing intentions to others that they did not have, drawing the wrong conclusions, and ignoring forecasts with arrogance and superficiality.

There are also little-known shortcomings in the international system. For example, while mechanisms for consultation between the European Union and the Atlantic Alliance on strategic issues are solidly in place, the dialogue between the organizations and among the member countries always has been a challenging one, complicated by loyalties to the two organizations that are not entirely compatible. This is something to be perplexed about, since it clearly contradicts common sense. To take just one frustrating example, these two powerful organizations are hostage to the dispute over Cyprus! On the NATO side, Ankara does not want Nicosia sitting at the table for discussions between the two organizations. On the EU side, Turkey's request to exclude an EU member country from the table is not acceptable. The result is that nothing is discussed together, except operations decided before the EU enlargement of 2004, which included the accession of Cyprus. However, the Secretary General and the High Representative of the EU have recently agreed on cooperation in various areas.

The goal of the international community should be to move towards some kind of common architecture, but today we sense a return to bilateralism, characterized by the fragmentation of actors, little solidarity, and an instinctive distrust that must be overcome each time. International organizations, beginning with the United Nations, suffer from these problems and are therefore weakened. Added to this situation is the decline of the Old World, including Europe, and the emergence of new players unaccustomed to a dialogue among multiple voices, to forging consensus, and still unprepared to assume shared responsibilities.

Then there are peoples who are emerging from centuries of isolation and have never been independent. What can be done to connect them to the world that is moving on?

I fear that too little is being done. Greater willingness to reinforce international governance is needed, exactly what appears to be lacking at the moment. It is also true that we basically use a system born after World War II. But men are not naturally inclined to reform themselves, unless events force them to do so.

The Transformation of the Alliance

There is an old saying attributed to Lord Ismay, the first secretary general of NATO, according to which the Alliance was founded "to keep the Americans in, the Russians out, and the Germans down." George Robertson added mischievously "and with the British on top."

Lord Robertson used to spend weekends in Scotland and, when necessary, I had to deal with whatever came up. I remember the conclusion of a sensitive negotiation in late 2002, regulating the modalities for transfer of NATO "capabilities" to the European Union for its autonomous military operations. The Secretary General left saying: "Don't worry, nothing will happen this weekend."

Instead, the North Atlantic Council had to meet several times during that weekend. The European Union Summit, convened in the meantime in Copenhagen, awaited our conclusions in order to make its own decisions. It cost me a couple of very agitated phone calls with Javier Solana, High Representative for Common Foreign and Security Policy, the EU's de facto foreign minister and a tireless advocate for Europe, who also knew NATO very thoroughly. After many anxious moments, I successfully managed to conclude the negotiations with the agreement of the member countries; the British ambassador, Emyr Jones-Perry, was of great assistance, discreetly arbitrating between the Greeks and Turks. He advised me to end formally the meeting as soon as I had read the final agreed text, to avoid obstacles at the last minute.

This highly detailed agreement, usually referred to as "Berlin Plus," is certainly a milestone in the complex and difficult history of NATO-EU cooperation. The political significance is undeniable, and, from a practical point of view, it allows the two organizations to avoid duplicating capabilities and hence wasting resources. Berlin Plus is fundamental for Operation Althea, the EU-led peacekeeping operation in Bosnia-Herzegovina that succeeded NATO's SFOR in 2004. It is, however, the only example of this model of cooperation between NATO and the EU.

In fact, the Berlin Plus agreement did not put an end to institutional rivalry between the two organizations. At a certain point in 2003, for example, Lord Robertson tasked me to coordinate NATO-EU relations, seemingly at the encouragement of Emyr Jones-Perry, the very able British permanent representative (who was also a fine gentleman). I tried several times to establish personal contact with Robert Cooper, a distinguished British diplomat and intellectual, at that time Director General for External and Politico-Military Affairs for the EU Council. Every time a meeting was set, however, at the last minute there was an "unforeseen" problem on the other side. Clearly my interlocutor had no intention of meeting with me.

At a certain point, I felt the need to inform Emyr, who otherwise may have thought I was not active enough on this issue. He was angry and frustrated when I explained the situation. The result was a phone call of polite apology from the other side of Brussels, but the substance of NATO-EU relations did not change. (Clearly there also were different views within the British system.)

In fairness, the Atlantic Alliance remains, by its very nature, highly traditional, like the other historic alliances we studied at school. However, unlike other alliances in history, NATO's distinguishing feature is that it was not dissolved once the objective was achieved. Instead, it has become a permanent structure.

Unlike the European Union, NATO makes no pretense of being supranational. It has a minimal budget that covers the costs of running its central administrative bodies. Otherwise, it relies completely on the human and financial resources of its member nations, including for public diplomacy. Since the end of the Cold War, there has been much talk about transformation and a new headquarters has been built.

For several decades, NATO was the West's point of reference, the security framework that made European development possible. Before taking up my position at NATO, I went to see Javier Solana, who had been Secretary General of NATO from 1995 to 1999, just before taking on his European Union responsibilities. He told me very politely that I was getting a good deal: the level of its staff was first rate, inasmuch as NATO was the only institution able to handle an international crisis.

NATO tradition requires that the most sensitive discussions take place in the format of informal business lunches among the permanent representatives. This is a practical system, enabling agreements to be reached on an informal basis. If there are differences, as is very often the case, these remain at an unofficial level.

Libya, however, was a special case. Lack of time meant that things were done too quickly for such a difficult decision, with the negative result that there was only partial participation by NATO governments in the operation.

The absence of NATO offices abroad is particularly significant for those forced to go on missions in remote areas. It is not easy to establish a direct link with counterparts in faraway places, and it sometimes is necessary to go through other channels, such as their embassies in Brussels. However, in these cases there is no guarantee that the messages will be faithfully transmitted, and neither is it easy to understand the true power and influence in capitals of their representatives in Brussels.

Member countries are selected on a rotating basis to act as contact points in various capitals. However, after a challenging mission in a distant country, it is somewhat burdensome to brief the ambassador of the contact point country, who is frequently not aware of the background for the mission. I remember, for example, my first briefing to the Norwegian ambassador in Amman. Coming out of the meeting, he informed me in all sincerity that Oslo did not send him staff, and as a result he was able to follow local events only up to a certain point.

A current theme is the relationship between civil society and the military. NATO is considered by some as a military organization, but that is not really so, since civilian control is its basic principle. In this connection, it is worth mentioning an incident in December 2006, when I went to Belgrade to open the Alliance's military office. Then President of Serbia Boris Tadić, invited me to dinner, along with the American admiral who was commander of Allied Forces South (AFSOUTH) in Naples. In the view of the Serbian president, the admiral was the guest of honor, but it was the admiral himself who changed seats at the table, knowing that the NATO deputy secretary general took precedence over him, and demonstrating the principle of civilian control over the military.

What can be done when the international situation changes quickly? Bureaucracies react with difficulty when leaps forward have been made and they are called upon to do unfamiliar things. The Alliance has remained in the foreground since the end of the Cold War, and has sought to transform itself via new military and technological capabilities. "Capability, capability, capability! " was Lord Robertson's watchword, the same used by Tony Blair to justify the creation of a European defense identity after the Kosovo campaign demonstrated the serious shortcomings of the European armies. However, no great steps were taken in this direction, and defense budgets continued to decline inexorably over the years, although the 2014 commitment by the NATO countries to spend at least 2% of their GDP on defense may help improve matters. At the NATO Summits in Warsaw (July 2016) and in Brussels (May 2017), member countries reaffirmed that pledge.

After the demise of the Soviet Union, Eastern European countries saw membership in the Atlantic Alliance as their priority objective, even before the European Union. For these countries, joining NATO meant protection from any future aggression on the part of Moscow. In addition, becoming a member of this prestigious club completely changed their image. This enabled inexperienced, newly established democratic governments to open up to the world.

In 2003, however, the Afghanistan "trap" forced the Alliance to act in a completely new environment. Without a doubt, the passage of time has weakened NATO's basic cohesion and transatlantic solidarity. This is no surprise, since, inevitably, the more the area of activity is widened, the more political cohesion is weakened.

In June 2011, US Defense Secretary Robert Gates criticized NATO. Actually, when he was saying NATO, he was addressing Europe for its insufficient attention to defense budgets. We are in a paradoxical situation, where in Washington the term Atlantic Alliance means Europe, and in Europe it makes people automatically think of the United States.

One day George Robertson told me about a long ago visit from Lord Carrington, an aristocrat of the old school, who had been NATO Secretary General in the 1980s. George said Carrington asked him: "How are things going? Is the restaurant as awful as it was in my day? And is the number two still an Italian?" In response to Robertson's affirmative reply to both questions, Carrington said: "It is a good sign, it means that things are still going well."

Today, however, governments have the illusion of being able to move better alone. To preserve an impression of solidarity and satisfy the political needs of the moment, the Alliance was forced to dive into Afghanistan and Libya and had to get by with inadequate resources and a mediocre consensus in a profoundly changed international situation.

Europe's Telephone Number

Little has been said about the European Union, although the topic would seem natural in connection with the Mediterranean, if not the Arabian Gulf. An explanation is needed.

Many years ago, Kissinger asked a now well-known rhetorical question: If I have to talk to Europe, what number should I call? Today, there is a telephone number, but Kissinger would not know who would answer on the other end.

During the Cold War, Western Europe delegated its security to the United States and NATO, which eased Europe's road to prosperity. The basic DNA for the construction of the EU thus concerned the single market, agriculture, and cohesion policies. It had nothing to do with military affairs, and very little with foreign policy. Exhausted by two bloody world wars and the Cold War, Europeans enthusiastically greeted the outbreak of peace, in their hearts saying "no more war."

The question of autonomy in the political-military field only began to be seriously raised at the end of 1998. French President Jacques Chirac believed the time had come for Europe to rid itself of American tutelage. The European Union's February 2001 Treaty of Nice sanctioned the birth of permanent European political-military bodies in Brussels, roughly reproducing NATO's functional framework. Everyone interpreted this event in their own way. London tried to convince the Americans that this would increase the Continent's military capacity. Paris chased its dream of taking charge of European Defense, which would allow it to deal with the United States on equal terms. There were major steps forward until 2009, when the EU's Treaty of Lisbon came into force, but with too many expectations.

As a founding member of the European Union's Political and Security Committee, beginning with the first meeting on March 1, 2000, I remember the initial difficulties. Even the European Parliament did not understand very much about this, taking issue extensively with Javier Solana, EU High Representative for Foreign Affairs and Security Policy, and demanding to see all of his communications. Poor Solana tried in vain to explain that every government has information that it does not disclose, and that this does not imply a lack of respect for institutions.

Arriving at the Justus Lipsius building for the first meeting of European Union ministers of defense, I overheard some ushers talking to each other, wondering if a movie was being filmed there. The reason? A German admiral in uniform had been seen taking the elevator, and the ushers were unaccustomed to seeing military personnel, since the EU until that time had no role in defense and security policy.

Therefore, you can easily understand that it will take years of experience before the defense institutions established by Europe truly become fully effective. In the world, the EU is broadly seen as being of great importance, but not yet in political-military terms.

To briefly complete the round of international institutions, the United Nations has always had great political legitimacy, but little practical effect. The best example was Bosnia in the 1990s. Because of the lack of directives, the UN forces were passive witnesses to massacres carried out under their very eyes. Srebrenica was the emblematic case, where a Dutch battalion helplessly witnessed the massacre of civilians by General Mladić, the Bosnian Serb military leader. It will never be easy to make an organization of almost two hundred countries function.

In concluding this long digression dedicated to multilateralism, my firm view is that, despite its complexities, it remains an achievement to be defended with conviction, as it represents a more advanced system for managing relations among sovereign states. We must not forget that the rapid growth of European society after the Second World War was largely due to the international institutions created in those years. They have given us more than two generations of peace and prosperity in Europe, benefiting the United States as well. An achievement that is unequalled in history.

www.ingramcontent.com/pod-product-compliance
Lightning Source LLC
Chambersburg PA
CBHW020610270326
41927CB00005B/263